The
Autistic
Trans
Guide
to Life

of related interest

Uncomfortable Labels
My Life as a Gay Autistic Trans Woman
Laura Kate Dale
ISBN 978 1 78592 587 0
eISBN 978 1 78592 588 7

Trans and Autistic
Stories from Life at the Intersection
Noah Adams and Bridget Liang
ISBN 978 1 78592 484 2
eISBN 978 1 78450 875 3

Trans Teen Survival Guide
Owl Fisher and Fox Fisher
ISBN 978 1 78592 341 8
eISBN 978 1 78450 662 9

The Awesome Autistic Go-To Guide
A Practical Handbook for Autistic Teens and Tweens
Yenn Purkis and Tanya Masterman
Foreword by Emma Goodall
Illustrated by Glynn Masterman
ISBN 978 1 78775 316 7
eISBN 978 1 78775 317 4

The Autistic Trans Guide to Life

Yenn Purkis & Wenn Lawson

Foreword by Dr Emma Goodall

Jessica Kingsley Publishers
London and Philadelphia

First published in Great Britain in 2021 by Jessica Kingsley Publishers
An Hachette Company

1

Copyright © Yenn Purkis and Wenn Lawson 2021
Foreword copyright © Dr Emma Goodall 2021

Trigger warning: This book mentions anxiety, gender dysphoria, suicide and trauma.

A CIP catalogue record for this title is available from the
British Library and the Library of Congress

ISBN 978 1 78775 391 4
eISBN 978 1 78775 392 1

Printed and bound in the United Kingdom by Clays Ltd

Jessica Kingsley Publishers' policy is to use papers that are natural,
renewable and recyclable products and made from wood grown in sustainable forests. The logging and manufacturing processes are expected to
conform to the environmental regulations of the country of origin.

Jessica Kingsley Publishers
Carmelite House
50 Victoria Embankment
London EC4Y 0DZ

www.jkp.com

Contents

Chapter 3 Coming Out   85

Foreword

This is a beautiful, moving and practical book that blends personal stories with the research literature to present evidence-based and lived experience strategies for living well as a trans or non-binary autistic individual. Case studies, poetry and the sharing of personal stories by the authors are juxtaposed with evidence from current research in the areas of autism and gender diversity.

The premise of this book is a powerful idea: that people can be more content and engaged with life if they are true to themselves in safe environments. This idea gives hope to some of the most vulnerable people in our society – those who are both gender diverse and autistic. The intersectionality of belonging to two groups, both of whom are frequently misunderstood by wider society and often stigmatized, is recognized but not dwelled on. Instead, the authors provide a road map to working out what your authentic self is and how you might express that in safe and authentic ways.

I have a passion for providing autistics with useful and practical advice across a range of areas, including sexuality and relationships. In doing this, I have researched the area extensively and come to realize there is very little quality information out there for autistics who are questioning and/or diverse in their gender and/or sexuality. This book fills that gap nicely and will be a great resource for autistics and their families, as well as professionals with whom they seek to walk along their journey of self-discovery and authentic expression of self. The evidence-based explanations around the different ways that us autistics express ourselves are both helpful to me as a professional and as a parent and a wife.

As an autistic cis-female, I have not experienced the depth of distress and joy expressed in Wenn's and Yenn's journeys, but I can attest to the autistic lived experience of not noticing, not being interested in and not following stereotypical gender 'norms'. As a child, I was a tomboy, a nerd and finally a geek. As an adult, I dress for comfort, which may be 'girly dresses' and 'flat shoes' or stretchy pants and shirts/blouses. Gender is so much more than the way we dress, it is how we feel about and describe our relationship with our bodies and minds.

I encourage you to dip in and out of this book and to savour each part, giving yourself time to process the thoughts and feelings being shared and ponder how this relates to you or someone you are supporting. It will be an emotional experience, but I am convinced it will be healing and helpful for all those gender-diverse and gender-questioning people seeking hope that they too can live a good life, whether or not they are autistic.

Dr Emma Goodall, autism consultant

Acknowledgements

From Yenn

I would like to acknowledge my co-author, Wenn. I have known of Wenn's work for a very long time and respected all he has given the autistic community and the wider world. Wenn has been a bit of a hero to me for many years. I feel honoured that Wenn agreed to co-write this book. It has been an absolute pleasure working with him.

I would also like to acknowledge Jessica Kingsley Publishers for publishing this book, which I hope will make a difference for a lot of people.

I would also like to acknowledge my parents, Glenys and John, for their significant role in my journey and for being respectful and welcoming of me as I am throughout my journey.

From Wenn

First, I'd like to acknowledge my co-author Yenn. Yenn and I have been mates for several years. We were both living in the same state in Australia, but hadn't met each other until 2005. We were also both diagnosed with autism in 1994, but by different clinicians. Neither of us knew that one day we would be sharing a gender journey as autistic and transgender people, Yenn as non-binary and me as transmasculine. If it weren't for Yenn inviting me to share in the writing of this book, my exploration of gender and autism would not have taken me on the more extensive journey of discovery that it has. Thanks Yenn!

I also wish to acknowledge my wife Beatrice who is my constant companion and champion! Accompanying me on my trans journey has been a very challenging journey for Beatrice, who has also needed to question her own gender identity. She tells me she has entertained the idea of having a male chest because she thinks it would suit her! But this is more a statement of fact rather than actually wanting to transition from one gender to another.

I acknowledge and thank my children (Guy, Katy and Tim) for their full acceptance of who I am and in having to change the way they see their 'Mum'. I don't think they could have envisioned their mother as a 'man mum' with a beard and a tattooed chest!

I thank our publishers for their patience in waiting for us to finish this manuscript so they could make it available as the book you are reading. Sometimes, as autistics, we battle low energy levels and executive functioning issues that cause us to take longer over completing things. We usually choose to do things we are interested in, but even these can be hard yakka!

Thank you to you, our readers, for looking into the pages of this book. We hope it is useful as well as informative.

Introduction

Hello, our names are Yenn and Wenn and we want to introduce ourselves as the authors of this book and to let you know more about our personal stories as trans and autistic adults.

Wenn

I was diagnosed as autistic in 1994, when I was 42 years old.

I knew I was transmasculine in 2013, when I was 61 years old. *I grew up a girl and became the man I now am.*

CONNECTING TO ME

I have my pen knife in my side pocket,
The fire flames crackle; the damp wood spits,
As Autumn dampness around me sits.
I hear the squirrels, a distant owl,
For evening approaches and dreams warm my soul.

I stand in the corridor, the train window pulled down,
A journey that puffs from village to town.
I study by day and church claims the night,
The hours of listening, of learning about 'right'.
I love the bell ringing and in the choir singing,
Beginning to notice; my inside voices' plight.

Creating a life; movement ahoy,
pink for a girl and blue for a boy.
So much love and so much pain,
It's like I am born all over again.

Connecting to self and noticing 'Other',
I'm someone's sister; I'm someone's brother.
My body dictates all these different states.
I cannot 'feel' the sense of what's 'real',
They both seem to own me,
They compete for a place.
Finally home; my heart can now see.
So I can now welcome, all that is me.

What was your journey to an autism diagnosis like?

My journey to diagnoses was fraught with confusion, misdiagnosis (intellectual disability, schizophrenia), depression and lots of misunderstanding of my behaviour. Finding medical professionals who understood what was happening to me was elusive. I spent 25 years in and out of mental health facilities with years of antipsychotic medications and other medicines, such as SSRIs (selective serotonin reuptake inhibitors) for anxiety and depression. I was over 40 years old when I finally had an appropriate assessment for autism.

What is being an autistic person like for you?

This is a strange question because I only know myself as me. So, being autistic is 'normal' for me. I can't imagine myself any other way. I sometimes wish I didn't have the difficulties that I do, but I wouldn't give up being me, and these difficulties along with my strengths (that autism gives me) are part and parcel of who I am.

What are you writing about in this book on autism and gender identity?

In this book I and my co-author are specifically writing about autism and gender dysphoria and gender identity in autism. There are as many gender identities as there are other differences between people. Gender dysphoria (a mismatch between the gender you were assigned at birth and the one(s) you feel at home in) in autism is only starting to become understood.

What would you say is key to understanding gender dysphoria in autistic people?

Gender dysphoria (GD) in autism doesn't necessarily have only one explanation. However, the key message is that if we don't take this seriously, up to 40 per cent or more of our population will be living with such discomfort, confusion of self-identity, poor mental health, difficulties focusing at school and at work, and incredible struggles fitting into traditional gender roles, or a total disregard for social norms/expectations, that suicidality seems like their only option. So, the key message here is one of 'listen and act or the opportunity for that person to live a connected and meaningful life might be totally and permanently lost'.

What are the specific difficulties of being an autistic
person experiencing gender dysphoria?

Again, specific difficulties for autistic GD individuals will
vary. These range from a belief that they should be free to be
themselves (e.g. a 6-foot-tall bearded male with a deep voice
seeing no reason that they can't walk down the high street
in a dress, because they know they are female) without any
need to medically or socially transition; to an individual long-
ing to socially and medically transition into the appearance
and outer shell of the gender they know themselves to be
but don't have family or financial support to do so. There are
also many other hurdles to get over, such as not coping with
invasive medical tests due to sensory discomforts. So, there
are environmental, social, personal, family, religious, physical
and financial challenges, let alone finding an accepting community where 'whoever you are' you are welcome and can take
time to discover and grow into being yourself.

Do you agree with recent research that suggests
gender identity variance and gender dysphoria may
be more prevalent in the autistic population?

It does seem likely, for many reasons, that GD is more common
in autism. This doesn't mean they are joined at the hip! When
you consider our honesty, our preponderance for truth and
fairness, then gender identity is likely to be more fluid and less
binary. Why do we need to fit into a mode of social expectation
if we truly don't believe this is who we are? The non-autistic
world is governed by social and traditional expectations, but we
may not notice these or fail to see them as important. This frees
us up to connect more readily with our true gender.

*How can autistic people best be supported
in exploring their gender identity?*

Each person is different. It depends on their personality, sensory sensitivities, family and education, financial and personal access to services and so on. First, we need to be listened to, heard, and then appropriate accommodations need to be made for us. This might mean doing nothing apart from listening, watching and observing to build a fuller understanding of the bigger picture (e.g. is this an obsession with the other gender, is it a sensory discomfort/ like, is it a phase or interest; or are they telling us that this is who they are?). Alternatively, it might be paramount to act more quickly. For example, some young people need puberty blockers to give them time to process issues regarding gender dysphoria. Delaying puberty actually gives everyone time to explore options. If a young person is on the way to puberty, and they are telling you they are transgender, then joining a gender clinic or being placed in a specialist setting to gain access to appropriate 'treatment' is essential. Once a young person's voice changes and they become taller and start sprouting a beard, it's very difficult to undo it. For young trans boys, having to go through menstruation and grow breasts can be an absolute nightmare. So, listening to the individual, working together, acceptance and becoming informed, joining specialist provision and following expert advice, taking things one step at a time, and so on, are all ways to support the unveiling of gender identity for those who question their gender.

*What key advice would you give to professionals
when supporting autistic people experiencing gender
dysphoria or exploring their gender identity?*

Professionals should make sure they are well informed of the
topic and the issues regarding autism and gender dysphoria.
Being neurodivergent rather than typical has a different impact
on this scenario and these people may need different handling
from the rest of the population. The whole process of gender
discovery can mean there is a need to give information in an
autism-friendly format. For example, I was unaware of some
of the challenges I would need to face when I transitioned.
No one explained the sensory and emotional process to me,
only the mechanical one. I think this was because even if the
general social and medical transition process is explained
it's put in the format of details relevant for the non-autistic
population. For example, I didn't know that with a penis
and standing to pee I would literally be in the line of scent
and would therefore notice the fragrance of urine. It was helpful to know that urine smells less strong if I drink more water.
There are many other issues like this to detail for different
individuals at different stages of exploration. Professionals
need to be ahead of the game!

*Why do you think it's important to share your story
about your personal experience of gender dysphoria?*

We all have a story to tell and each of our stories will be different. I think it's important to share my personal story because
having autistic role models and others who have gone ahead
of you lets others know some of what it might be like for
them. I wished I had had people to read about, to talk to and
share with who might have understood me and who would

have been available to connect with. I learned so much from YouTube videos of the transgender experience. But there is a danger that if we don't go through appropriate channels, we may be opening ourselves up to wrong and misleading information. We need to counter ignorance and myth with reality and honesty in ways that increase support and make a difference.

How is autism perceived in Australia?

I think Australia is highly aware of autism, especially through all the TV and media that is out there today. But, awareness and action are different things. We speak too easily of inclusion without really understanding that real inclusion means accommodating an individual with all the right means to enable them to become all they can be. This can't happen traditionally with traditional teaching because this doesn't suit the learning styles of autistic people. Once Australia catches on to what inclusion really means, it will tell a different story. We are closer than ever, but still not close enough.

What's the one thing you want people to get?

The one thing I'd like people to take away from this is that gender is a spectrum, just like autism. This is not a linear line which goes from male to female, it's not set in stone. Gender is a spectrum that incorporates many differences of experience, not just binary ones. A spectrum that houses differences from 'I'm not any gender, I'm me' to 'I'm male at the moment'; 'I'm female today'; 'I'm male'; 'I'm female'; 'I was born with a female- or male-looking body but my brain is the opposite or my brain is both or my brain isn't set that way' is the evolving reality of gender. So, please listen and work with us, step by step, a little or a lot at any one time. I need you to hear me and help me sift through this confusion; walk with me, not behind or in front, just with me.

Yenn[1]

I was diagnosed with Asperger syndrome in 1994 at the age of 20 and was among the first adults (like Wenn) to be diagnosed in Australia. I didn't accept my diagnosis for a further seven years and even then it was quite a tentative acceptance. I really found my autistic identity when I wrote my autobiography, *Finding a Different Kind of Normal*, in 2005. I became an advocate for autistic people and families, and advocacy became my passion.

In terms of gender identity, I have always felt that I sit outside the male/female binary and that I occupy a sort of third gender option but there was no language for this until I was well into adulthood. I came out as non-binary in 2018 and it was a huge liberation. I felt a similar level of pride and respect as I had when I accepted my autism. I was instantly a very proud non-binary person. As part of my transition, I took on my they/them pronouns and after a while changed my name – both of which were very affirming acts. I felt largely accepted and welcomed by the LGBTQIA+ (lesbian, gay, bisexual, transgender, queer, intersex and asexual) community and was excited by my discovery of who I am.

As an advocate with quite a large reach, I found myself having the opportunity to influence the autism world. Part of this was very liberating but part was highly frustrating as I discovered that there is a lot of bigotry and trolling around

1   See my website at www.yennpurkis.com

gender. On one occasion, I posted a video diary about my coming out on YouTube. It attracted dozens of trolls calling me all manner of transphobic insults. I discovered that gender is apparently a hot topic for trolls. It didn't discourage me from posting material about gender but it did make me wary of posting things if I was feeling a bit fragile.

There is a community of trans and gender-diverse autistic people which I am very honoured to be part of. A lot of autistic young people are now coming out as trans and this fills me with joy. I hope my advocacy can make a difference for the next generation of trans and gender-diverse autistic young people and children.

'My name is Yenn: Affirming gender, affirming self'

One Monday I was at work, sitting at my desk, when what I can only call a flash of inspiration hit me. In less than the time it took you to read the last sentence I found my name and I knew my name was Yenn.

I think I'd better backtrack a bit. Since 2018, when I publicly affirmed that I was non-binary in my gender, it has been an amazing time of self-discovery and reflection. My old name, Jeanette, is about as gender loaded as you can get. I have had conversations with a friend called Bernadette and we both concluded our names were quite strongly suggestive of the feminine. When I came out, I wondered if I should change my name. I started thinking about it but nothing worked. I concluded that I would know when I knew. And I did. The only convincing I needed when 'Yenn' popped into my brain that Monday was to see what it looked like written down. I tried

it with an 'e' on the end which didn't look right. I tried it as
'Yenn' and I knew I had found my name.

I considered where it had come from and realized it has
a few 'parents', thoughts-wise. The main thing I see is poetry.
To yen in poetry means yearning, or as I see it, aspiration and
personal reflection – both things I have a lot of experience of.
It is also a little nod to my old, Jeanette name and it is quite
individual. Written, it looks strong and complete. Spoken, it
sounds confident and passionate. It might seem like a very
quick decision but it was the culmination of a lot of reflection
over the past few months.

When I knew my name, I knew I also needed to tell friends.
I sent a message to a bunch of close friends and emailed my
parents. I said, 'I will take this gradually...', and then realized I
do not 'do' gradual, so on my way home from work I changed
the title of my social media pages to Yenn Purkis and posted
a message about why I had done this. I had experienced a lot
of transphobia and trolling over the past few months, so I was
caught between liberation at my new me and terror that people would attack me. Thankfully, I have not had any negative
responses and nobody unfriended me on social media that I
am aware of, out of almost 10,000 people on Facebook and
5000 on Twitter. That Monday, I spent the afternoon and
evening in a state of joy.

A few days later I heard my name spoken for the first
time, incidentally by author Graeme Simsion as I was part
of a launch event for his new book. He said 'Yenn' and then
smiled and told me I didn't immediately look around! It took
a while for me to respond, given that I was new to it as well.

I am fairly certain there will be people who will not like
my new name due to its connectedness to my gender identity.

There are quite a few transphobic bigots in the world, even in the autism world, sadly. I have had people say 'I thought this page was about autism, not gender' and insist any commentary I make stays on the autism topic only. To me though, gender diversity and autism are fairly clearly linked with so many of us being trans and gender diverse. This is not just my anecdotal evidence either, there is a lot of research evidence which demonstrates this too. I am here as an advocate for autistic and trans and gender-diverse people alike and I would much rather be a visible gender-diverse person if that helps others who feel they cannot come out themselves and are experiencing bigotry of self-hatred and doubt.

I am becoming acutely aware of why it is referred to as 'transition' and not change. I really, really wish I could make a decision about my identity and expression and magically everything would change that needed to, but it doesn't work like that. The legacy – writings about a gender I no longer identify with, my name changing across documents and profiles, people using my pronouns – these things really get to me. I just want it all done now. Maybe the need to wait and change things more slowly than I would want is what my mum would call 'good for your soul'? Not sure.

The response I have had to my new name has been overwhelmingly beautiful – people I don't know at an event telling me what a lovely name it is, a colleague at work that I came out to giving me a card which said 'this calls for confetti' and had a really meaningful message that she had written, my boss telling me I had her full support and was available should I need her despite being busy, almost 500 people liking or reacting to my Facebook post about my new name, all the people saying 'Hi Yenn!' and 'Your name is beautiful', the organizations changing my name on their promotional material for upcoming talks. This affirmation is so overwhelmingly lovely and was not really expected. I keep expecting hatred but there has been none, quite the opposite in fact. I really wish this was the case for everyone affirming gender.

So I am a new me. My old Jeanette name never really fitted to my mind. It feels as if I was wearing a big old coat that didn't quite fit right and was uncomfortable, but it never occurred to me to take it off until I did and now I am in a metaphorical jacket that fits just right and looks good to me and others and allows me to move freely and express myself the way I want to.

I might say that these things do not come without doubts and insecurity and lots of questioning, but within that there is somehow a great certainty as well.

I like my new me. That was an important week for me, so I wanted to share it with you all as well.

CHAPTER 1

Autism and
Gender Identity

This book is a survival guide for trans and gender-diverse autistic adults. The authors, both trans and gender-diverse autistic people, feel that such a book is needed and wish such a resource had been available to them at several points on their own journeys. The book covers a range of topics and is a survival guide for navigating life well as a trans/gender-diverse autistic person. It includes practical advice based on the authors' personal knowledge and academic research. The book is inclusive and respectful and comes from a strong position of pride.

Autism is widely misunderstood, and although it impacts individuals in so many differing ways, it's becoming apparent there may be a variety of profiles that may even seem contradictory, but actually are all part of individual autism. We need to write and speak about these because they impact on your gender and transition journeys. For example, how can you be autistic but find that structure and rules evoke more anxiety rather than less? (Traditionally autistic individuals have been thought to thrive best when structure and rules are provided.) However, the traditional understanding of autism has changed dramatically over time. Once autism was thought to be a male thing, then it was thought autism did occur in females, but only rarely. Over time this became a ratio of four to one, males to females, while more recent studies suggest it's two or three to one (Loomes, Hull & Mandy, 2017). So, autism has differing profiles, is just as common in females as it is in males and occurs across all populations at a current rate of around 1 in 58.[1]

This information is important when assisting us in our understanding of gender differences, gender dysphoria and transgender issues because it gives a wider perspective on the developing history (herstory and theirstory) of autism over time, and on our understanding of autism over time. Also, is there more gender dysphoria and gender diversity in autism than in the general population? The answer is, most likely (Furfaro, 2019).

A good video to watch that explains gender dysphoria and possibly how it develops can be found in Michael Mosley's BBC documentary, *Countdown to Life* (Episode 2).[2]

Autism profiles

Going back to autism profiles though, we want to give you an idea of how these may impact our understanding of our gender discovery journey. First, let us dispel some myths. It's been hard to understand some behaviours seen in autism (e.g. the

1 www.autism.org.uk/about/what-is/myths-facts-stats.aspx
2 www.dailymotion.com/video/x38hzm7

need for many to have routine and structure but the need for others not to) and these might impact our gender journey. Are you feeling 'pulled and pushed' but are finding it hard to make a decision, even though you want to? It might be because your particular autism profile includes an avoidant disposition which has been wrongly accredited as being oppositional.

If this is you, we hope the following information, which paints a picture of the differences between extreme demand avoidance and oppositional defiant disorder, will help. This is important to us because sometimes when as autistic individuals we insist on our need to transition but then we don't find it easy to 'conform' to the expected journey, it maybe because our autism profile includes massive anxiety leading us towards the need to avoid. This doesn't make our gender identity less valid, but it does add a layer of complexity and, as we learn to understand this, it's easier to be kind to ourselves.

Julie is 18 and has been living as a trans person for four years. However, Julie (6 feet tall, very big and unshaven) insists on wearing dresses and wigs. But Julie won't (or can't) change any other aspect of herself nor can she tolerate the idea of hormone treatment. She avoids going to any clinics for support and gets aggressive towards those who try to support her. Julie's family have suggested her gender identity is just another obsession and possibly related in some way to sensory dysphoria.

It may be that Julie is autistic, trans and has pathological demand avoidance (PDA). Let us explain. PDA is one type of autism profile where individuals experience any type of expectation as a demand that increases anxiety beyond being able to cope. Although extreme demand avoidance (EDA) as a diagnosis does not yet exist within the *Diagnostic and Statistical*

Manual of Mental Disorders, DSM-5 (American Psychiatric Association, 2013), there are existing guidelines for assessment of PDA and it is a very real issue. Also, it's becoming increasingly likely that this will figure in future editions of diagnostic manuals.[3]

Incorporating an understanding of EDA or PDA[4] (also known as persistent demand avoidance) into our appreciation of individual journeys is imperative because it gives us another lens to view our lives through to help us make sense of why, at times, for some of us there is this pull towards something we know we need or are and an equal pull to avoid it. The competing pressures can cause us to hide or howl (fawn, fight and flight and so on).

Currently, research shows that:

∞ EDA/PDA co-exists with autism (Gillberg *et al.*, 2015; Newson, Le Marechal & David, 2003; O'Nions *et al.*, 2014a, 2014b, 2016) and is thought to be a particular autistic cognitive style and profile born from anxiety/ trauma that is pathological/biological in origin (O'Nions *et al.*, 2014b). The main characteristics that separate PDA in autism from oppositional defiant disorder are explained below.

∞ Oppositional defiant disorder is a childhood disorder defined by a pattern of hostile, disobedient and defiant behaviours directed at adults or authority figures characterized by angry and irritable moods as well as argumentative and vindictive behaviours

---

3   See Gillberg's commentary at https://onlinelibrary.wiley.com/doi/full/10.1111/jcpp.12275
4   www.autismwestmidlands.org.uk/wp-content/uploads/2017/11/PDA-1.pdf

purposely aimed at annoying others and causing conflict, while placing the blame on others for this behaviour (e.g. Ghosh, Ray & Basu, 2017). This disorder does not come from an overwhelming need to avoid demand.

In autism, we see a set of behaviours showing restrictive interests and communication differences arising from a brain hardwired to allow individuals to experience life via single focused attention. This gives rise to a spectrum of differences in social ability (American Psychiatric Association, 2013; Lawson, 2000, 2011; Murray, Lesser & Lawson, 2005). This will mean environments and situations requiring multi-focused attention – doing more than one thing at any one time (e.g. listening and writing; looking and listening; eating and sitting; thinking and listening) – might lead to disabling of individuals. In turn, this leads to autistic individuals experiencing delays and differences in social and communication areas, with outcomes seen as rigid behaviour restricted interests and social imagination, and communication differences (leading to disability due to environments that don't cater for autistic dispositions). However, autism also represents itself through an individual's personality (e.g. shy, outgoing), their cultural disposition (their ethnicity; being deaf or blind; having physical disability, etc.) and whether they have co-occurring challenges (e.g. attention deficit hyperactivity disorder); specific learning challenges (reading, writing and arithmetic); mental health challenges; language delays; dyspraxia, and so on. All of the above is also filtered through an individual's family upbringing, beliefs and traditional norms. These include gender expectations placed on individuals, sometimes even before birth.

Therefore, autism is multi-dimensional, meaning individual profiles can vary considerably depending on the combination of the above factors and a person's strengths and difficulties across these two key dimensions:

∞ How someone relates socially.

∞ The need for sameness, often resulting in repetitive or rigid thoughts and behaviours, or coming from a different cognitive style.[5]

When it comes to how people cope with pressure and demand, this is also an individual thing. Very often in our ancestry there was trauma. It might have been from parents or grandparents experiencing World War II or other wars. It might be from an ancestry such as First Nations People in Australia, America, Canada and so on, where families were divided, children stolen, lands taken away and so on, or it might have been from a family's exposure to domestic violence, poverty, poor mental health and so on. Whatever the reason, most of us have intergenerational trauma in our background. Research shows that this can have a profound impact on our own identity today (Gravitz, 2018). This doesn't easily go away and often presents as post-traumatic stress disorder (PTSD). So, in our journey of gender discovery, these components will also impact on us and it's not always easy to separate them out.

---

5   www.youtube.com/watch?v=A1AUdaH-EPM

EDA/PDA characteristics

∞ Resisting and avoiding the ordinary demands of life, which might include getting up, joining a family activity or other day-to-day suggestions. This may be the case even when the person seems to want to do what has been suggested.

∞ Using social strategies as part of the avoidance, for example distracting, giving excuses, rather than simply ignoring, refusing or withdrawing.

∞ Appearing sociable on the surface (e.g. people with EDA may have a more socially standard use of eye contact or conversational skills than others on the autism spectrum), but lacking depth in their understanding (e.g. not seeing a difference between themselves and an authority figure).

∞ Excessive mood swings and impulsivity, sometimes described as a Jekyll and Hyde type scenario or that they go from 0 to 100, in two seconds.

∞ Being comfortable in role-play and pretence, sometimes to an extreme extent and often in a controlling fashion. This may be a means of trying to cope with their own anxiety or avoidance demands (e.g. some children role-playing may say something like 'I can't pick that up because I'm a tractor and tractors don't have hands').

∞ 'Obsessive' behaviour that is often focused on other people, which can make relationships very tricky.

People with an EDA profile can appear to have better social understanding and communication skills than some other autistic people and are often able to use this to their advantage. However, these apparent social abilities can often mask difficulty with processing and understanding communication and social situations. When avoiding demand becomes an extreme need, some individuals will use extreme measures including profane language, aggression and hostility. Their behaviour is outside their control, because it is a biological response to perceived threat, and is likened to that of a cornered rat! So, should we ignore this? No, we simply need to find better ways to reduce demand and help individuals feel safe.

The outstanding differences between oppositional defiant disorder and PDA are in the core nature of the avoiding behaviour which is extreme but not intended to cause conflict and annoy others simply for the sake of it. It is innate and comes from a disposition, trauma induced, to fight demand which is experienced as anxiety provoking to the point of 'meltdown' and sometimes catatonia (e.g. Craig, Trundle & Stringer, 2017).[6, 7]

The above understanding can impact our gender journey and this is why the information is crucial. We have met autistic individuals with varying profiles, there is no 'one size fits all'. It's important to know yourself and your profile so this can be factored into your gender experience.

---

6   www.youtube.com/watch?v=0gCXwBh2saQ
7   Guidelines for PDA can be found at: www.autism.org.uk/about/what-is/pda.aspx

Trans and gender diverse

Please note that the terms 'trans' and 'gender diverse' will be used interchangeably in this book to describe trans and gender-diverse people. Identity-first language will be used (e.g. 'I am autistic' rather than 'I have autism'). The authors are both proponents of autistic pride, LGBTQIA+ pride and neurodiversity. This is not a book about 'fixing' autistic people or trying to make people conform or 'pass'. It is a book about navigating life well, as you are, with pride in yourself as a gender-diverse autistic person.

The book is written from a perspective of empowerment and acceptance. It has a strong focus on promoting self-worth and positive self-knowledge. It is focused on practical advice and support, including stories of personal reflection, which are included as case examples throughout the book.

Practical tips and advice can be found throughout the book which address a range of topics, including what gender diversity is, having the 'coming out' conversation in different contexts, the life elements of work and study (including sample transitioning guidelines for the workplace), renting property, intimate relationships and relationships with family and children, and information on self-advocacy.

The information within this book is for adults (young and older) and, as such, reflects the reality that a lot of trans people often 'come out' later in life. To the authors' knowledge, the book is the first of its kind for autistic trans people and is aimed at autistic people exclusively.

Being full of useful advice from a trans and autistic perspective, this book should assist you to navigate life well, understand yourself better and manage difficult situations such as coming out to family or work colleagues. The book is written to empower and encourage trans and gender-diverse autistic people to be their authentic selves.

Gender diversity

Transgender people are individuals of any age whose gender identity and expression does not conform to norms and expectations traditionally associated with their 'sex' assigned at birth. It is important to note that not all transgender people want to undergo sex reassignment surgery and not all require or want to initiate hormone therapy.[8]

The World Professional Association for Transgender Health (WPATH)'s guidelines (in summary) state that even in areas with limited resources and training opportunities, health care providers can apply many of the core principles that underpin its Standards of Care. These include the following:

∞ Show respect for clients with nonconforming gender identities and do not pathologize differences in gender identity or expression.

∞ Provide care (or refer to knowledgeable colleagues) that affirms the gender identity of the client, and reduces the distress of gender dysphoria, when present.

∞ Become knowledgeable about the health care needs of transsexual, transgender and gender nonconforming people, including the benefits and risks of treatment options for gender dysphoria.

---

8   www.ippf.org/sites/default/files/ippf_imap_transgender.pdf

∞ Match the treatment approach to the specific needs of clients, particularly their goals for gender expression and their need for relief from gender dysphoria.

∞ Facilitate access to appropriate care.

∞ Obtain the informed consent of clients before providing treatment.

∞ Offer continuity of care.

∞ Be prepared to support and advocate for clients within their families and communities (schools, workplaces and other settings).

Autism, gender and the non-autistic population

In today's age, we commonly talk about inclusion and acceptance. School, college and university life are tough on most of us but, due to autism being seen as a social disability, it's even tougher on autistic individuals, as well as those who teach us, those who support us and those who learn with us. The social curriculum is one most non-autistic individuals learn almost by osmosis, while autistic individuals find this very difficult. Why is it so hard? Why are friendship, concepts of public and private, your stuff, my stuff and daily awareness of 'other' just not on the radar of some autistic individuals? We could blame autism for our difficulties, but this would be short-sighted. We know it's not simply being autistic that impedes us or interrupts our ability to relate to self and to others, it's also the environment we are in and whether or not who we are is being accommodated.

It seems clear that when another person is 'different' to oneself, that difference can pose a threat. Autism alone is viewed by many as a form of mental illness or cognitive deficiency, which of course it isn't! For some, autism may co-occur with many other issues, which may include cognitive delays, learning difficulties, physical ailments and mental health issues. But, these are all common to non-autistic individuals too. However, for those of us on the autism spectrum, our communication 'means' may differ from the non-autistic population. For example, some of us don't use speech as our means of communication – we may type, use visuals, sign, use speech and no gestures or use both, but avoid eye contact, and so on. This difference in how we communicate causes discomfort among those in the non-autistic population, who may not be familiar with us! Unfortunately, though, their discomfort may cause them to judge us as being less able than we might be or not in a position to make decisions about our lives that they view as being complex. All of the above impact negatively on building friendships and can make it difficult to form relationships, unless we have lots in common with each other. So, sharing similar values and interests is often the way to navigate friendships and other trusting relationships. This book should help to give you confidence to challenge many of the misconceptions around such things as autistics lacking empathy or autistics not wanting friends, and so on. As we build confidence in ourselves, we will find it easier to be friendly. Also, relating to those who 'get us' is a huge part of enabling success in our friendships.

Gender and *sexuality* are different things. Gender represents your innermost 'knowing' of where you belong on the gender continuum. Sexuality is about who you are attracted to sexually. Both gender and sexuality may be experienced differently by the autistic population when compared with the non-autistic population. In autism, our brain enables us to function best when it accesses information via single-focused attention, one thing at any one time. This makes traditional socializing very uncomfortable because, in general, social interactions require the use of multi-dimensional attention (e.g. looking and listening and even moving all at the same time). This has implications for gender and sexual development. To date, the research on gender and sexuality in autism is scanty. Some research suggests pathways to autism in men and pathways to autism in women are different but that there will be some overlap. Although the concept of a masculinized brain in autism is still being debated, gender differences in autism may also impact gender identity (Lai Meng-Chuan, Lombardo & Baron-Cohen, 2013).

The idea that males and females experience sexuality and gender differently in autism is not new, but it does mean that there is a need to look at individuals and their differing profiles for individual development of sexual and gender identities as well as how to support us in our diversity. We do not believe there is 'male and female' autism, but we do believe autism presents differently in different people. We note that females, for a variety of reasons, have often been overlooked. This has negatively impacted the numbers of autistic people in any population because women have not figured in the research. It might also be that gender identity and gender fluidity in autism hasn't been fully appreciated. Sometimes gender and sensory discomforts have given a confusing picture, and these need to be separated out so we can truly decide what belongs where. It is hoped this book will help you find your place and also assist you in this process.

CHAPTER 2

Gender Diversity, Affirming Gender and Transitioning

Introduction

This chapter focuses on what is meant by gender diversity, and gender differences in autism. It illuminates the different kinds of diverse identities there are. Consideration is given to these in association with autism and gender diversity and what it means to be trans and gender diverse and autistic. Topics such as common myths and misconceptions, definitions of gender diversity and what is involved in gender affirmation will be dealt with in detail in this chapter, providing an understanding of gender diversity and identity. The chapter also provides detailed information on the social, medical and legal aspects of transition. The themes illustrated in this chapter are continued throughout further chapters too. This is because so many of those in this chapter overlap with those in other chapters.

What is gender?

Historically, in the English-speaking world, gender has been presented as a binding disposition, either male or female, as assigned at birth. However, in today's world these options do not accurately represent the experience and identity of a great many people. In 2014, Facebook introduced 58 options for gender for users of its site. While 58 was a good start, it could be argued that gender is an individual consideration meaning there are around 7 billion genders, each one specific to each human being. Identity is a very personal thing and each person's understanding of their gender will differ from the next.

Gender, as well as being biologically determined, is a societal concept which, like a number of things, is socially constructed. This applies to traditional roles in relationships, gendered interests, expression, preferences for activities, employment roles and even preferences for foods. Society has clearly defined roles for different genders and there are expectations based on gender which cross into all aspects of life.

So, gender diversity is about the association of difference in identity, but it's written about in this book as it relates to us across the gender and autism spectrum.

Gender transition/affirmation

Gender transition is about identifying as a different gender to the one you were assigned at birth. Before transitioning from one gender to another, some people experience gender dysphoria, a sense of distress where the gender a person is assigned at birth does not match their actual gender experience of who they feel they are. Transgender people can experience gender dysphoria but it is not a necessary attribute in order for a person to be transgender.

Gender and autism

There are frilly, girly girls, there are tomboy girls, there are girls who like woodwork, hairdressing, gardening, cooking – there's a huge spectrum that's female. This is also true for boys. But, there are also girls who wish they were boys, and boys who know they're really meant to be girls, as well as those who feel their gender is 50/50, 25/75 and so on. It's an incredibly strong thing. But it can take longer for some of us to connect the dots, especially if we are autistic. Some of the figures showing in autism research suggest gender dysphoria and other gender and sexuality issues are higher within the autistic population. Gender dysphoria individuals are living with extreme discomfort and the literature states around 40 per cent attempt suicide (Adams, Hitomi & Moody, 2017; Bailey, Ellis & McNeil, 2014). Poor mental health among our population is higher than for any other and must not be ignored. In the *Diagnostic and Statistical Manual of Mental Health* (American Psychiatric Association, 2013), gender dysphoria is understood as a biological condition, rather than a psychological one. The treatment for this biological condition is to transition from one gender to the other as concurred by the individual concerned.

❝ {WENN} So, there are a great many different gender identities. Gender is often one of the most deeply held parts of a person's identity. For autistic people who are trans and gender diverse, the relevance of gender and identity is likely to be heightened even further.

I know when the light went on for me and I knew I was

'male', though living in a female body at the time, transitioning from female to male was all I could think about. It consumed me day and night. I watched every YouTube video I could find, googled gender dysphoria and read every journal article I could. I was so taken over by my discovery I even forgot to eat! When one person said they thought it might be a phase I was going through, like some of my other passions, it was hard to know how to answer them. I knew within myself I had stumbled on the reason I was never quite at home. But how do you know if you are never allowed to become acquainted with your true self? I had to do my research, yes, and also trust myself to make the right decision. 〞

This is what can happen for us because, as autistic people, we tend to be passionate about what captures our interest. This is one of the reasons others may find it hard to believe us when we say we want to transition or we no longer want to be known by the pronouns given to us at birth. Maybe there was always evidence of this in our growing up, but it's equally true we might not have been unhappy before the light went on.

People who are trans and gender diverse face significant discrimination in society. This is likely due in part to the gendered expectations in society and how trans and gender-diverse people transcend and challenge these. Despite this discrimination, trans and gender-diverse identities are valid, and discrimination is the thing which is wrong. People have the right to identify and express gender in the way/s which are right for them.

Different gender identities

Transgender/LGBTQIA+ advocacy group GLAAD defines transgender as:

> An umbrella term for people whose gender identity and/or gender expression differs from what is typically associated with the sex they were assigned at birth. People under the transgender umbrella may describe themselves using one or more of a wide variety of terms – including transgender. Use the descriptive term preferred by the person. Many transgender people are prescribed hormones by their doctors to bring their bodies into alignment with their gender identity. Some undergo surgery as well. But not all transgender people can or will take those steps, and a transgender identity is not dependent on physical appearance or medical procedures.[1]

Some identities within the trans umbrella include trans man, trans woman, female to male, male to female, trans male and trans female. There is no set way to 'be trans' and each person will have their own experiences. Trans does not need to be a singular identity and some trans people identify with additional identities such as non-binary or gender fluid.

There are many different aspects of gender identity. You may identify with one or more of them or you may identify with something different. A selection of identities are outlined below.

---

[1]   www.glaad.org/transgender/transfaq

Non-binary

Non-binary simply means having a gender which is outside the male/female binary. Non-binary people may identify as a number of genders or as having no gender. Non-binary is an umbrella term under which sit a number of different identities. Non-binary people may use they/them pronouns, but some use he/him, she/her or a combination. For some non-binary people, identity fluctuates, while others may express themselves differently on different occasions. Furthermore, for some their expression is more consistent. One of the authors of this book is non-binary and has experienced several significant changes to their gender identity and expression over the years.

Genderqueer

Genderqueer is a similar term to non-binary identity. Genderqueer means not subscribing to binary male or female distinctions and identifying as neither, both, or a combination of male and female genders.

Demiboy

A demiboy is someone whose gender identity is only partly male, regardless of their assigned gender at birth. They may also identify as another gender in addition to feeling partially male, such as identifying as non-binary or trans.

Demigirl

A demigirl is someone who partially, but not wholly, identifies as a woman, girl or as being feminine, regardless of their assigned gender at birth. They may or may not identify as another gender in addition to feeling partially feminine, such as non-binary or trans.

Neutrois

Neutrois describes a person who identifies as neutral or having no gender, being neither male or female. This can be associated with gender dysphoria or not.

Gender fluid

Gender fluid is an identity under the non-binary and trans umbrella that means a person's gender is fluid and can change.

Gender nonconforming

Gender nonconforming describes a person who does not conform to social 'norms' or expectations of gender expression. Being gender nonconforming does not mean a person needs to be trans or non-binary but it is often the case that they are. Gender nonconforming can be seen as more a measure of expression than identity in itself but could also relate to gender identity.

Gender questioning

Gender questioning means a person is questioning their gender identity. They may go on to identify as trans and gender diverse or they may not. It is important for people questioning their gender to be provided with support and respect so that they can reach an understanding of which is right for them. Questioning does not need to be something which happens once. Many people go through an ongoing process of questioning throughout their life.

Pangender

Pangender means identifying as more than one gender. Pangender people may be all genders or both the binary genders of male and female. Pangender people often use they/them pronouns.

Autism and gender diversity – intersectionality

For reasons which are not completely understood, autistic people are considerably more likely to be trans and gender diverse than the general population. This means that within the autistic community there are a lot of trans and gender-diverse people, and within the trans and gender-diverse community there are a lot of autistics (Nobili *et al.*, 2018).[2]

Autistic people who are trans and gender diverse experience intersectional disadvantage. Intersectionality is a concept which can describe the experience of disadvantage due to having or being associated with more than one area of discrimination. It is defined by some as: 'The complex, cumulative manner in which the effects of different forms of discrimination combine, overlap, or intersect.'[3]

---

2   www.eurekalert.org/pub_releases/2019-07/aru-sft071619.php
3   www.merriam-webster.com/words-at-play/intersectionality-meaning

Imagine first that there are a number of groups of people in society who experience discrimination, prejudice and exploitation – such as people of colour, LGBTQIA+ people, disabled people, indigenous peoples, people from culturally and linguistically diverse backgrounds, women, people with mental illness, those caught up in the criminal justice system and those from low socio-economic backgrounds, to name a few. Membership of any of these groups results in disadvantage and inequality. If you belong to more than one group, the disadvantage is compounded or multiplied. It is not like being a little bit more disadvantaged but more about becoming disadvantaged in a complex way.

The converse of disadvantage is privilege. Privilege is experienced by white people, cisgendered heterosexual men and wealthy or middle-class people. Privilege doesn't necessarily mean that these people will have an easy life. What it means is that they won't have to work extra hard to achieve things society assumes everyone should be able. to, but which disadvantaged people have barriers to, such as employment and education. It is not in essence 'bad' to be privileged. The negative part of privilege happens when people fail to be aware that they are privileged and assume that others who are disadvantaged are 'not trying hard enough'. A commentator who has a number of areas of privilege once said that autistic people who are unemployed should 'get off their butts and get a job'. That is clearly a statement based in privilege. That commentator would be better advised to consider the reason autistic people struggle to find work rather than judging them.

Put simply, an autistic person who is trans and gender diverse is experiencing intersectional disadvantage. If this applies to you it can be a useful way of understanding how society works in this particular realm. It also implies a need to be kinder to yourself if you are having a difficult time.

Autism and gender diversity – what the research says

At the time of writing this book there is minimal research into autism and gender diversity. However, the research to date suggests gender diversity, gender variance and gender questioning are more common among the autistic population (Strang *et al.*, 2014, 2018; Van Der Miesen, Hurley & De Vries, 2016). It also reports that poorer mental health and a lack of appropriate support for autistics are prevalent. For example, Cassidy (2015) reports suicidality is higher in general, within the autistic population, so coupled with gender variance which is not understood or accommodated, autistic individuals will feel less supported and experience higher levels of anxiety and depression.

At least if we understand what might be happening to us, we can sort out which aspects of discomfort might be due to sensitivity towards a heightened or underactive sensory system or other types of sensory dysphoria, or due to personality, or due to gender variance and gender dysphoria or due to autism!

Common experiences for trans and gender-diverse autistic people

While all autistic people are different, there are some similar experiences for trans and gender-diverse autistic people. Sadly, many of these relate to negative experiences like bigotry or being denied access to medical procedures supporting transition.

Some common experiences include:

∞ Having a sense of being different, often from a young age (but not necessarily attributing these feelings to gender).

∞ Being bullied due to autism or gender.

∞ Having difficulties accessing medical procedures.

∞ Being dismissed and invalidated by medical professionals.

∞ Having gender identity doubted or invalidated by others.

∞ Feeling a strong sense of pride as an autistic person and a gender-diverse person.

∞ Feeling connected to the autism and/or trans communities.

∞ Having resilience and determination.

∞ Being patronized.

∞ Facing assumptions that a person is cisgender and asexual.

∞ Facing challenges accessing education and employment.

∞ Facing discrimination in employment.

An important part of listing these common experiences is that it reiterates that you are not alone. There are countless other autistic and trans and gender-diverse people who have similar challenges and experiences. It is important to note that the challenges in this list are almost exclusively related to how society responds to us and treats us rather than any inherent deficiencies in our character or selves. This book focuses on some of the more negative experiences listed here and provides insight into some ways to address them.

Common myths and misconceptions

There are a number of myths and misconceptions about trans and gender-diverse autistic people. These include:

∞ Gender diversity is a phase or 'obsession' which will somehow 'resolve' in time. This means that autistics are often denied access to medical procedures such as hormones and surgery because it is believed that they will change their mind. This idea of phases or obsessions which pass in time is not borne out in the evidence around gender diversity and autism (Stagg & Vincent, 2019; Strang, 2018).

∞ Autistic people can't be self-aware or have an understanding of their own gender.

∞ Autistic people are all cisgender and asexual. This view is often used in relation to any disabled people and particularly people with intellectual disability. It is ableism and is highly unhelpful and invalidating to disabled people.

∞ Autism can be evidenced in the extreme male brain theory, which is not the same as extreme maleness.[4] The misperceptions resulting from this theory can negatively impact gender expression.

∞ Trans autistic people don't/shouldn't have children. Trans and gender-diverse autistic people actually do have children. This is not a negative thing, and judging parents based on their gender or neurotype is highly problematic and also insulting.

Considerations about sexuality, sex and gender

It is very common for people to conflate sexual/romantic attraction and gender as if they were the same thing. However, sexuality and gender are quite separate things. Sexuality is about who you are sexually and romantically attracted to. Gender is about how you feel in terms of your gender identity. You can be a transgender person with many different ways of experiencing sexual and romantic attraction. Because your gender and sexuality are different things, one does

---

4   https://theconversation.com/extreme-male-brain-theory-of-autism-confirmed-in-large-new-study-and-no-it-doesnt-mean-autistic-people-lack-empathy-or-are-more-male-106800

not necessarily impact the other. Non-binary people with androgynous expression are not necessarily gay or lesbian, just as cisgender people are not necessarily all heterosexual. This is a very important consideration and one which needs to be shared and understood widely. But because gender and sexuality are not really connected and are distinctly different elements of human experience, it does not necessarily follow that this is understood in general terms.

Adults and children

One of the major differences in the adult autistic population, when compared with that of autistic children, is that the brain may have developed more in some areas due to brain plasticity. For some, this allows adults to recognize faces more, but not interpret them, have a lower sensory threshold (rather than higher) and be prone to greater fear. It's therefore imperative that we have named others who can support us appropriately.

66 {WENN} When I went for surgery my wife came with me. She was great at all the support things I needed, such as taking care of shopping, laundry and checking in on my emotional and physical needs. 99

Navigating all the processes of gender transition alone, even the social ones, can be very difficult. Finding someone to share all of this with, whatever your journey, is very important. For example, having a trusted friend who can tell you (because you've given them permission to) the lipstick colour you have chosen doesn't go with your outfit and the outfit is a size too small is very useful, especially if they can help you choose more wisely.

Sensory issues

There can be sensory issues attached to affirming gender. For example, 'male' designated toilets can have a strong smell.

66 {WENN} There were some sensory differences that might have become issues for me if I hadn't had some help. For example, I didn't expect post-surgery, when I stood to pee, that I would find the smell of my urine overwhelming and hard to deal with. Part of the simple answer was to drink more water, which dilutes the urine, is better for your kidneys, and lessens the smell.

As a trans guy I needed to learn how to shave. I found the whole experience very difficult to navigate. Should I use an electric shaver or get used to wet shaving with a razor? If I use a razor, which direction do I shave in? When I asked some cis-guy mates, they each had a different opinion. This made it difficult for me to make decisions, so I decided not to shave and to let my beard grow. I had promised my wife I would remain clean shaven, so I needed to chat with her about this. She said I should go for it and not worry. So this is what I did. I seemed to take a very long time though! Four years later I had a decent beard. The feeling of hair growing on my face was strange and it took some time to get used to. I have chosen to have a wet shave at times, just to keep my beard tidy. But, I also use an electric shaver which I can adjust the cutting size of so I can make sure the beard is even (as much as is possible). I found the uneven growth on my face uncomfortable because I like everything to be even! When I looked at other guys, though, I noticed their beards weren't even and most men looked untidy, with some whiskers being longer than others. 🙶

For trans women, there can be many sensory discomforts they need to adjust to. For example, wearing women's underwear that doesn't fit very well (especially pre-surgery), the feel of make-up and the scent of lotions and potions! We just need to remember it takes time to get used to these things. If you find taking time over something isn't easy, try to structure your time so you can check in often, but not too often. For example, you could video yourself every three or six months so you can see the changes. Many of us want it all to happen straightaway. Learning to be patient is an asset, and it's the only way to go.

Body changes

If we have come late to an understanding of our gender dysphoria and a desire for gender transition, the chances are we are already fully grown and have our adult body. If this is the case then puberty-blocking hormones might not be of any use. For some, the advice is to live in our chosen gender for a minimum of 12 months before embarking on any kind of hormone therapy. This might mean wearing the chosen clothing and hairstyle and so on that fit your idea of your chosen gender identity, so beginning the journey of social change but not the medical one. Some might argue that being an adult we already have made our decision and don't need the 'practice' run at living in our chosen gender and we should be able to move towards the medical transition, if we want to, straightaway.

66 {WENN} I really was uncomfortable with the idea that I needed to 'prove' to others that my gender transition was real and I wasn't going to change my mind. However, although I didn't like it, I did find it useful to know I could freely dress as I wished, without feeling the pressure to conform to the gender I was assigned at birth. The whole process also slowed me down and gave me thinking space, which was beneficial. Of course, WPATH, which provides clinical guidelines to professionals to assist transsexual, transgender and gender nonconforming individuals towards becoming the person they are happy and comfortable with, has stated that consent to medically transition, from a therapist who knows the individual, alleviates the need for a surgeon to feel qualified to make such a decision. Maybe it's not so much a process of 'gatekeeping' but more one of an ethical model before surgery.

Once surgery happens and parts of our body are removed and reshaped, this is forever. I have not once missed the breasts I had nor regretted the removal of every other 'female' part of me. But some may wish to keep parts of themselves, choosing to do so for personal reasons. Whichever way you decide is best for you is fine. You are in charge of your body, and having partial surgical gender-affirming surgery, full gender-affirming surgery or no surgery at all is your decision and does not impact on your gender identity. Your gender identity is not about your body parts, it's about being at home with the right gender identity for you.

Some trans individuals choose to bind their chests to keep themselves looking flat chested so they fit more the male image. Some trans individuals use padded bras to feel more at home as a female. It's important you feel comfortable with yourself and with what you choose to do. As autistics though, we can get very obsessed with these things and they can completely take over our lives. I'm not sure what might help us here, except to say if this really bothers you, it might be time to ask yourself if you would be better off having the surgical procedure that best suits your needs, so you can move on and live your life without constantly being taken up with the appearance of your body.

I have to say, though, that even after surgery you might still wrestle with the question of whether or not your chest/breasts are what you hoped for! I'm very happy with my chest 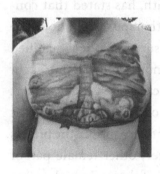 but I did still feel uncomfortable that my scars were visible. I tried for two years to 'dull down' this visibility by using scar creams and tape, but it didn't really make a difference. I also had the scars treated by laser treatment, three times, but that didn't help either! In the end, I had my chest tattooed. I love the tattoo and I'm very happy with my chest now. So much so I can go bare-chested with confidence. I will probably have more tattoos around my sides and back, not so much that they are necessary but more because I like tattoos! 〞

〝 {YENN} I have a binder which I wear when I feel the need to. I love the way it makes me feel and love wearing dresses with it because it makes me feel like a young man in drag. There are some down sides to binding and you have to be careful not to injure your back by wearing the wrong-sized binder. I bought mine online. I have considered 'packing' (wearing a prosthetic penis) but haven't done so yet. I like playing with my identity and seeing how different expressions make me feel. I often wear my binder to work. It makes me feel nice. I am looking into having top surgery which would mean I don't need to wear my binder and would be boyish all the time. 〞

When it comes to what sex affirmation surgery you might have, if you choose to, there are a number of different surgeries and techniques on offer. Making sure you fully check these out and are well informed before you make any decision is vital. Wenn not only google checked everything, but also watched YouTube videos posted by other trans men, checked the medical sites of doctors, explored what medical insurance would cover and so on.

Knowing what's out there, what your preference might be and what the implications are is so important. For example, some surgeries require a process of stages that take up to three years, while others are completed in one hit. Some mean several weeks before you can return to work, others need a few months. Knowing when to book a surgery is also important. For example, if you are advised to wear limited clothing it might be best to have such a procedure when the weather is kinder or you can guarantee you will be somewhere warm.

〝 {WENN} As an older person having surgery presented other risks, such as increased risk for blood clots, so I needed to think about pressure stockings and anti-blood clotting medication. 〞

If you choose to travel abroad to access surgery, it's important to fully check out all the details of what might be covered, for example who books the flights and accommodation? How long will you be in the country for, and do you need a visa? It's also important to add on extra time, because too often a wound might break down, an infection might occur and so on. If the hospital recommends two weeks, allow yourself three!

How do you envisage your gender identity?

If you think you are non-binary in your gender, do you want to look more androgynous? Do you have days you prefer typical women's clothing (a dress, a skirt, a ball gown, a blouse and so on), with high heel shoes? Then you have other days you want to hang around in clumpy boots, jeans and a shirt? These are usual feelings for a non-binary person. It might seem confusing and contradictory but actually you are being true to yourself. If others comment on this and say things like 'Can't you make your mind up, which one is you?', you can genuinely respond, 'They both are.' In everyday life, all of us, whatever our gender, wear clothes to reflect our mood, the day, who we are with and where we are going, but the non-binary person might feel as comfortable in formal male wear as in formal female wear and the same for situations that are informal. It may not depend on the place, the people or the occasion as much as it does on who you are on that day. This doesn't mean you are more than one person; you are you. But the 'you' is not bound to any particular gender expression so much as it is to being the expression of the gender you are. Others may find this difficult to understand because they are used to being one fixed gender (male or female) and find it hard to comprehend that someone can be a gender that is not fixed for them.

You may feel very much at home in a fixed gender that is not the gender you were assigned at birth. Your physical body on the outside may look female but you are actually male, or vice versa. So, taking your male self and wearing it on the outside of who you are (matching inside to outside) will be new to you and you may need to experiment with what feels right for you. It could be the type of haircut you get, the clothing you wear, if you bind your chest or not and so on.

66 {YENN} My gender expression changes every day. I often wear skirts and jewellery but I also often wear jeans, a 'man's' t-shirt and boots. I wear a binder some days and make-up other days. I feel like I get the chance to play around with my gender expression depending on how I feel. It is liberating. I don't shave my legs or armpits and my hair is very short and partially blue. I am as non-binary on the days when I wear 'girls" clothes as I am on those where I wear 'boys" clothes. 99

Female to male (FTM)

Very few of us will be able to change the body we were born with to access the body we most desire!

66 {WENN} I am only 161cm tall and as a female I didn't think much about my height. But now living as a male I think about it all the time! I have noticed that there are lots of males who are my height and it's not that unusual. But I still feel 'uncomfortable' and I wish I were taller. I even wear high insoles inside my shoes to give me an extra centimetre! I know it doesn't make much sense, right, but if it helps your self-esteem (my self-esteem) it's worth it. However, there are some things I will never be able to change. For example, I'll never be the 'muscle guy' with biceps like balloons and a 'six

pack' like those superheroes I watch in my science fiction shows. Of course, I'm like them on the inside of myself!

Over time, as I took testosterone, my voice changed – as will yours – and I love the deeper voice I now have. But while it was changing I went through those typical stages any person does during male puberty (I just did this as an older person rather than a younger one). This meant my voice didn't suddenly become deeper, it was gradual. Some days, my voice sounded like it was 'cracking' and it was scratchy. I understand now why people talk about the voice 'breaking'. This was a term I had found uncomfortable, even scary! Our voice doesn't really 'break', it deepens in sound due to the vocal cords thickening.

So, you might notice your voice seems lower on some occasions than it does on others. It might be your voice feels a bit 'squeaky' at times and a bit strange. This is all a usual part of the transition process.

I was worried about my 'singing voice' because in my female form I loved to sing and it was natural and easy for me. In my male form, since transitioning, my deeper voice finds it less easy to access the notes. I need to practise singing in a slightly higher key than seems to come naturally to me, and I have to remember this if I am singing publicly, like in a gathering!

To help aid my masculine appearance, I chose to grow a moustache and a beard. You might decide to do the same. If you do, it's important to remember that growing enough facial hair to look like a full moustache or beard takes time. Maybe you remember those youths 'back in the day' and the comments they endured from others as they were teased at the lack of facial hair on their still young adolescent chins! It could be the same for us. It usually takes between two and six months to grow a decent beard but that's dependent on where you are in your transition (it took me until year four on testosterone before my beard looked reasonable, but your adolescent self or puberty stage might be different from mine) and it depends on your genetics. I began to lose my head hair, even as a female, and my genetics appear to give me a pre-disposition towards baldness. This was even more evident during my transition. I cared about this in my female form but it doesn't bother me as a guy! If it bothers you, it's important to know you can help support head hair growth with the right shampoo and other pills and potions. You can speak to your GP about this to find out what they recommend. I also noticed that my physical strength increased, even without working out. 🙶

You might be the kind of individual who loves to work out and feels that exercise is very important to you. If you are, go for it! In whatever way, just being male gives you more muscle mass and more strength in general. For many of us, especially as older people, muscle mass is very helpful because being older and arthritic the muscle strength might help your physical body to feel stronger and more able. Even if you don't work out though, going for walks, using an exercise bike at home (while you watch your favourite show), walking whenever you can (taking the stairs, not the lift) and so on are important for physical health and well-being. Exercise has been shown to be as powerful a medium for good mental health as is an anti-depressant.

Male to female (MTF)

If you are transitioning from male to female, your height isn't something you can change either, but you might find yourself wishing you could be shorter! The good news is, even though you can't shrink your size, you can dress in ways that give you more of an elegant look. As you practise walking differently and adapting your gait to a more female stance, this will help you too. You might have some great female friends who can tell you how you are doing. It's important to accept their assistance with this because probably they can also help you with choosing the right clothing for your body shape. As people, all of us, whatever our gender, come in a variety of shapes and sizes and knowing how to dress and look our best (the best we choose, not the best for someone else) can help us feel good about ourselves. Sometimes we may really love a particular lipstick or eye shadow, but this might look great on others rather than on us.

Your voice

Changing the sound of your voice is harder for MTF individuals because changing the hormones in your body won't alter the physical structure of your vocal cords. You can practise speaking in higher octaves and a speech therapist can assist you with this. Finding a good speech therapist who understands your needs isn't always easy. It might be useful to check out your gender clinic or online support. Later in this chapter there are some websites listed that are helpful in explaining and showing what is achievable.

Unwanted hair

Rather than finding ways to encourage hair growth, you might want to discourage it. Shaving usually leaves a shadow over parts of your face and this might cause you to feel less feminine. Your face still won't feel as soft as you would like it to either; this might bother you, but using a good face cream and foundation can help disguise this. You might consider having laser treatment to remove unwanted facial and body hair. This can be very uncomfortable and expensive. If you choose this method, check out the credentials of the agency and make sure you are choosing well. You might like to use other ways to achieve unwanted hair removal. Your local chemist or pharmacy might recommend certain products. Usually on trans websites or forums much discussion about this and other issues takes place and you can get ideas about what worked for some and what didn't work. Ordering products online, which can work well for us, needs to be done with caution and always read the instructions carefully before trying any particular product. There can be very unwanted side effects from chemical products that cause irritation or allergic reactions.

Pre-surgery

If you are considering surgical intervention and wanting sex re-alignment you will be asked to have hair removal by laser. The surgeons (if local to you) should be able to recommend an appropriate specialist to go to for your treatment. If you can't find this information from your doctor, you could check with your gender clinic and seek advice from your online community, who might know more.

You might also want to explore what types of surgical intervention you are best suited for, can best afford, your health insurance might cover and so on. In Australia, there are only a few surgeons performing male to female genital surgery (bottom surgery), but having a male chest transformed into a female chest with the right size breast implants (top surgery) is more readily available. It's called 'bottom surgery' because it's referring to the lower half of a person, whereas 'top surgery' is all about the upper half of us!

There are many different types of both top and bottom surgery. Please be advised about these, compare your options and work out what you feel most comfortable with. There are lots of YouTube videos and blogs about individual experience. It's great if the surgeon has photographs on their home page or agency website. When you go to visit the surgeon, ask them as many questions as you need to. It's important to write your questions down and have them ready. No question or query is too small or too insignificant! This is your body and you need to know, step by step, what to expect. It can also help to take a friend you trust to the appointment.

Wenn's surgery experience

66 {WENN} I chose to travel overseas for my top surgery, to Brighton in the UK. However, at first I had an appointment in Australia, but chose not to follow through with it. I saw the surgeon there used drains after surgery and I couldn't imagine myself coping with those, so I found a surgeon in the UK who didn't use them. I'm very thankful to the plastic surgeon there who did a great job on my top surgery! I was heavy breasted

and needed a different type of surgery from someone with less breast tissue to remove.

I have lots of sensory issues and I was really worried about wearing a binder post-surgery. It's really important to wear one, if the surgeon says so, because it helps flatten the chest and also prevent blood clots. I found that lining the binder with cotton material (I cut up an old, very thin T-shirt) helped me to feel more comfortable. You might be fine without this, but I needed to do it. I'm also very thankful because my wife was with me all the way, helping me dress, prepare meals and even helping me with changing any dressings. I had to avoid simple things like lifting my arms up, so wearing clothing that zipped up so I didn't have to put it over my head and having pull-on pants was helpful.

For my lower surgery, I also travelled overseas because at that time Australia didn't perform lower FTM surgery. I chose to have a metoidioplasty[5] rather than a phalloplasty,[6] for several reasons. The first one was my worry I could lose sensation and I didn't want to risk that. I know several individuals who say they have not lost sensation and can happily still climax during sex, but I also knew the chances were lower, if you chose phalloplasty. The other reasons were the costs, which are more than double, and the time factor – surgery is often a ten-hour stint, and phalloplasty is a procedure that can be

---

5   Metoidioplasty, also known as meta, is a term used to describe surgical procedures that work with your existing genital tissue to form what is called a neophallus, or new penis. It can be performed on anyone with significant clitoral growth from the use of testosterone. Most doctors recommend being on testosterone therapy for one to two years before having metoidioplasty

6   Phalloplasty is the other most common form of lower surgery for trans and non-binary people. While the metoidioplasty works with existing tissue, phalloplasty takes a large skin graft from your arm, leg or torso and uses it to create a penis

undertaken in three stages over a couple of years, whereas metoidioplasty is usually one procedure that takes six or seven hours, then it's over. This includes having testicular implants too. Also, due to my age (I was 63) it was not recommended I have an anesthetic for up to ten hours, and then take a longer recovery time.

However, even having metoidioplasty can lead to problems, especially if you have a urethra hook up that allows you to pee through your penis! Fistulas[7] are common, and infection too. My second surgeon (I ended up needing a meta correction[8]) was amazing! After my initial meta didn't look the way I hoped and I lost my implants due to infection, I travelled to New Delhi in India, where the amazing Dr Kaushik[9] sorted me out. Of course, everyone's experience is different.

Although I cannot speak about first-hand experience of transition or surgery for male to female transition, I can share some information, both from observation and from what others are saying. 🙶

The quote below was taken from *The Girl's Guide to Changing your Gender* (Tourjeé, 2017):[10]

Hormone replacement therapy (HRT) is closely associated with the healthcare of transgender people. It is exactly what

---

7   A urinary fistula is an opening in the urethra that causes urine leakage. When metoidioplasty is performed with urethral lengthening, fistulas most commonly occur at the junction of the native and neourethra (although they can occur anywhere along the neourethra)

8   Meta correction is when a metoidioplasty develops complications (fistula) which need surgical intervention to fix

9   www.transhealthcare.org/narendra-kaushik

10   www.vice.com/en_us/article/43e899/male-to-female-transition-guide

it sounds like: replacing the hormones that are currently dominant in your body (if you're a trans woman, this is very likely testosterone) with hormones that are typically more prominent in the opposite sex (estrogen). For trans women, HRT typically comes in two parts: A medication to block testosterone in your endocrine system, and estrogen to replace it.

In case you didn't know: Estrogen works within the body whether you have a penis or a vagina. 'All bodies, regardless of sex assigned at birth, have the potential to react to hormones...estrogen will stimulate chest or breast growth in all bodies. Testosterone will stimulate muscle mass and facial/body hair growth in all bodies. The degree of change, however, is different for every person...penises tend to reduce in size once a person is on estrogen.'

In case you want evidence that biological sex is a big old myth even our 'male' genitalia bears traces of a previous sex: There is a scar going down the middle of the testicles. This scar is typically darker in color to the surrounding skin, and runs like a seam all the way toward the anus. It is called the perineal raphe, and is where the urogenital swellings fuse together in utero after the production of testosterone. If they hadn't fused, that tissue would be your labia; we're all female until we aren't... Regardless of our 'biological sex,' our bodies are produced from the same basic form, and they carry scars from long before birth to remind us of that.

Also:

'Hormone therapy usually achieves more masculinization or feminization if started earlier in puberty...once a body has been through puberty, there are often changes that hormones may not be able to completely reverse.' For trans women, these might include a deepened voice, facial hair, and masculinized facial bones. Nonetheless, HRT can have significant results on people well beyond puberty, including effects like breast development and fat redistribution.

And:

It's normal to be scared of going on hormones for the first time. As with any medication, only pursue it if you honestly believe that HRT can improve your quality of life. In my case, a few months after I started HRT, I felt better about myself... It felt empowering to take control over my body after many years of feeling like I was its victim.

MTF breast growth stages during transitioning

66 {WENN} Breasts are so fabulous they deserve their own section. Resources for trans breast expectations can be found at Second Type Woman[11] – The information was mostly written in the year 2000, but the website has some good material and also some images explaining the different stages that both breasts and nipples go through, once an individual is taking hormone replacements. This being also the most common process of breast development for cisgender women. Everyone is different though, some trans women grow large breasts, others do not. Remember once on HRT, you will experience

---

11   https://secondtypewoman.info

a second puberty. Breast development can be one of the first changes to occur during HRT. It's common that within the first two to three weeks of taking the first oestrogen pill, you will notice your nipples look and feel different. It's likely they will feel softer and more sensitive. Within a month or so, the breast 'bud' will grow underneath them.

You can get breast augmentation (surgery) if you want it and it's accessible to you. Again, I can only recommend Dr Kaushik at Olmec Clinic[12] in New Delhi, because of my own experience and what I witnessed for others.

Dr Kaushik has an amazing reputation among the trans community.[13] He was totally accepting of my autism and took all steps needed to accommodate me. This even included cooking my meals in his kitchen in his home. I'm a coeliac but I also eat very bland foods, nothing spicy or containing strong flavours. I tried McDonald's in New Delhi but their burgers (only chicken as beef is not available) were too spicy! 99

Wenn's gender dysphoria after surgery

66 {WENN} It's not that my autism and gender dysphoria were exchanged once I stepped fully into the gender appropriate for me, but being in the right gender illuminated and cleared away some of the debris that not being understood had caused. Once I could separate what was what, I found it much easier to own areas of difficulty, accept the support I needed, and move with confidence into my masculine identity.

---

12   www.transgendersurgeryworld.com
13   www.youtube.com/watch?v=TbHiZEqigQQ

My autism hasn't disappeared, but it's taken more of a step backwards because I'm not so disconnected.

It's been interesting to experience a growing confidence in ways I've not known before. For example, since finding my home in being male I am less ambivalent over daily decisions. I believe this is because I'm more 'joined up' and this is allowing me to know more of my own mind rather than being torn by the opinions of others. I still have times of indecision, but this is usually due to being overloaded by demand!

Autism and gender dysphoria and gender variance exist across a spectrum, each separate from the other. However, as well as for other reasons mentioned, they possibly occur more frequently together than in the typical population due to the autistic affinity with honesty. Our ability to possess a greater gender fluidity and a deeper connection to honesty that is not socially bound sets us free to be who we are. If we don't feel 'right', we are more likely to own up to this. The difficulty comes in putting names to our feelings and to our discombobulation and dysphoria.

Some might argue that autism means having a more masculinized brain, due to more testosterone in utero, and this explains the higher statistics for gender dysphoria. Although there is some evidence that autistic females may have a more extreme male brain (EMB), there isn't evidence that the same is true for autistic males (Lai *et al.*, 2013). Even so, how it impacts on the female brain is still being debated. We think that, however you look at it, EMB theory doesn't explain gender dysphoria or autism, as there are so many more variables!

When it comes to issues of gender dysphoria/transition, it appears there are more males transitioning to females than females to males. Again, this might be because, as autistics, we are not so bound by social rules of needing to conform and are freer to be ourselves. As for genetics and the role of hormones in issues of gender, there is no evidence either way that gender dysphoria being more prominent in autism is due to this. The research is in its infancy and there is much to explore. For me, the reasons are not important so much as having our stories heard. 🙷

Considerations for younger people – autistic and trans identity

Young autistic individuals often receive family support for the different ways they process information and for their differing learning styles (technology, visuals, role-play, music, etc.).

🙶 {WENN} Possibly due to growing up in the 1950s and 60s I wasn't given the interventions that now exist for young people. I was expected to muddle through on my own. Because I couldn't 'read' the hidden curriculum of social interaction I filled the gaps in my understanding with comic books and science fiction. Identifying as an alien or a mutant gave me a fictional population to belong to. I also loved certain television shows like *Lassie* and would imagine myself as the boy with his dog. I even dressed in jeans and baseball boots, just like the boy in the TV show.[14]

This felt right for me and today I believe this was more than simply identifying with a hero. It was an attempt to locate my gender identity. As an autistic child (undiagnosed at the

---

14   www.imdb.com/title/tt0046617

time) I was unclear about many things, including appropriate ways to communicate. I adopted an American accent and lived daily life as if I were that lad. Eventually, as an older person who was housed in a female body, I believed I was a 'butch' lesbian due to my affections for the female sex. I think it was forming this identity that kept me bound to the 'wrong' gender (for me) for such a long time. I never felt right using the label 'lesbian' but it was all I connected to at the time. "

" {YENN} As a young person, I had a very masculine gendered expression. I shaved my head and wore 'men's' clothes. I thought this meant I was a lesbian as I conflated gender and sexuality. I was usually thought to be a young man. I felt best when wearing 'masculine' clothes and liked that people thought I was a boy. I had no language for a non-binary gender identity as it simply didn't exist as an option then. As I grew older, my gender expression changed, and now I wear some 'masculine' clothes and bind my chest and also wear more 'feminine' clothes. I wish I had understood about gender diversity when I was a young person as it would have opened a whole world of possibilities and positive identity for me. "

Considerations for older autistics

As children, we may be able to get away with living as mutants, in a world we create, but as we become adults this is no longer tolerated by family or the society we live in. So, as we age, things can dramatically change.

" {WENN} Losing access to the way I identified due to it not being socially acceptable pushed me into deep depression.

Self-confidence fell through the holes in the fabric of my life and the demands of life outweighed my ability to cope. 99

This may account for the reasons some research shows that autistic adults fare poorly in the workforce and their sense of well-being is lower than that of the general population (Lever & Geurts, 2016). We can also see this happen for gender identity, in being confused about who we are. To date, there is little research on autism and gender identity to help us understand the inter-relationship they share. However, as we listen to other adults tell their stories, maybe we will get some clues. We know statistics on gender dysphoria appear to be higher in the adult autistic population, or those adults with autistic characteristics, by at least 6–7 per cent (Heylens *et al.*, 2018) compared with 1 per cent of the typical population. Identifying as trans isn't a one-time event. Coming out to ourselves is a process and may need to happen several times before it becomes our reality.

Affirming gender can be a process, as mentioned in the previous chapter. Coming to a place of knowledge, acceptance and contentment with one's gender is a journey. For some, it will mean a recognition they have been living in a state of misidentified gender and this is something they wish to change. So, for some, transitioning from one gender to another will involve a number of elements. Each person will have a different experience of transitioning or affirming their gender. As affirming gender means the process of becoming or stepping into your true or actualized identity, it also involves factors beyond self. Therefore, it is a process that happens over a period of time. The first step in affirming or moving into your discovered gender is usually becoming aware that you are transgender or gender diverse. The transition starts from this point. So, full development of one's affirmed gender often does not have a set end point, with many people's identity and their understanding of it continuing to evolve over time.

Elements of transition include:

∞ *Coming to a realization that you are trans/gender diverse.* This can take some time for a person to arrive at or it can happen quite quickly. Many experiences contribute to a person's understanding of their identity. Some awareness develops from discussion with other trans and gender-diverse people, especially friends or family members, awareness of gender diversity in media and popular culture, and much self-reflection. It's not so much that one thing turns a switch on, but many things coming together to form a picture that represents a truer sense of 'yourself', or 'selves'.

∞ *Coming out or making a public stand.* Coming out is not just one conversation. A person usually comes out on several occasions to several different people. A person might come out to family, friends, partner, children, work colleagues, people in the same clubs (e.g. sporting), health professionals and others. Each of these coming out conversations may be very different. Some will be harder than others. Coming out can be a liberating and empowering experience but it can also go badly, resulting in bigotry and transphobia.

∞ *Making changes in gender expression* (e.g. clothing, appearance).

∞ *Changing pronouns and titles.* Pronouns and titles are a key part of affirming identity. Changing to he, she or they in turn changes how a person views themselves and importantly how others view and relate to them. Pronouns reflect our understanding of a person's identity. Requesting and asserting the use of new pronouns is a core part of transition/affirming gender for many people.

∞ *Changing your name.* Possibly even more so than pronouns, changing their name is an assertion and positive affirmation of who a person is, their very core and identity. Changing your name can be viewed as a huge liberation, a new and more complete way of being. It takes some people time to find their new name, while others may have been using it internally for some time, but to affirm gender they then share it with others.

∞ *Making 'official' changes of names, pronouns and gender on official and other documents.*

∞ *Using the bathroom facilities which are appropriate for a person's identity.*

∞ *Advocacy and activism.* This is a part of affirming gender which many people become involved in. Given we live in a world where gender identity is

politicized and where trans and gender-diverse
people can be attacked for their gender identity,
advocacy and activism can be a very important part to
affirming gender.

It can help to have an ally or allies when travelling through
all the processes of affirming gender. Affirming gender can be
a difficult thing to do but also a liberating experience and an
essential step for many trans and gender-diverse people. As
autistic people tend to be very honest and upfront, we may be
quicker to begin the process of gender affirmation than our
neurotypical trans peers. For many, the process of affirming
gender may seem unreasonably long and they may wish the
transition to happen quickly. Others need a longer time to
work through the process and adjust to their new public
identity and expression as a trans person.

CASE EXAMPLE: KAI, AFFIRMING
GENDER THROUGH NAME CHANGE

*Kai is non-binary and autistic. They changed their name at the start
of the year. While Kai loves their new name and feels stronger in
their identity than ever before, they have not changed their name
on all their online accounts. Kai wants to do this but the process
for doing so is quite onerous on some sites, and every time they go to
do so they get distracted with something else. While changing their
social media and email accounts was done almost as soon as they
changed their name, these other accounts which nobody other than
Kai sees are not viewed as so important. However, Kai worries that
maybe not changing their name on everything makes Kai somehow*

'less trans' than they should be. However, as Kai is transgender, their gender isn't in question.

This feeling is real and very uncomfortable. It's part of the process of self-doubt. Seeing your chosen name on all your documentation takes time. Weathering the process in order to change things is important. Even after you think you have changed your name on everything, the 'old' name may still appear in places you might not have considered. In many ways, your current gender discovery has occurred via your previous gender expression. It's usual to want to ditch all and everything connected to the 'old' you. But, that person is still alive and well within you. They didn't die so much as reform, and the reboot and new you, who has always been there, will take time to exist as all of who you are. It is more like a reintegration of aspects of the gender you recognize, rather than only the one you were assigned at birth.

Changes in dress and expression

When people affirm gender, they may start wearing different clothes and change their appearance in other ways (e.g. wearing make-up, changing their hair). These outward changes can result in questions from peers. It can be very challenging to publicly change your gender expression, and transphobic bigotry can occur in relation to changes in expression. Like many parts of transition, changing expression and appearance can be very anxiety-provoking and very empowering at the same time. The anxiety element usually relates to society and the bigotry, ignorance, fear and hatred which some people live with concerning gender diversity. The anxiety does not necessarily relate to being transgender. It relates to being transgender in a world which often doesn't respect or care for transgender people and all that this involves for different gender perspectives.

66 {YENN} I wear a lot of different clothes, including sometimes wearing a dress over leggings and wearing jewellery. A friend made me a beautiful shiny rainbow dress for my birthday last year. I absolutely love this dress and took a selfie of me wearing it and posted it on social media. One of my followers commented that as I am non-binary I should not be wearing a dress as dresses are for girls. I felt very uncomfortable about this comment and worried I wasn't 'trans enough'. Thankfully, a lot of my social media family responded saying that a dress is neither male nor female and people of all genders wear dresses. I now feel happier about wearing dresses and jewellery and understand that gender is not determined solely by your expression. 99

Legal changes

Changing your name

Changing your name tends to happen in stages. First, you decide what your new name is. You may have known this for some time before sharing it with others or you may share it as soon as you arrive at it. Sometimes trying on a name will involve several changes until you are comfortable or at home with it. The next stage is telling others what your new name is and asking them to use it. This can happen all at once or over time. In the present day, you may have a lot of accounts and sites with your name on them, many not requiring a legal name change, such as social media accounts, online shopping sites and some workplace information. However, the next step is legally changing your name. This means that all your accounts can be changed to your correct name, including bank accounts, utility bills, licences and passport. Some people change all their accounts as soon as their name changes while others do so more gradually. Other than formal documents and accounts, the key stage of a name change is when you and those in your life exclusively use your correct name. Misgendering and 'dead naming' are rife and many trans and gender-diverse people accidentally dead name or misgender themselves for some time after transition due to the simple fact that they have used a certain name and pronouns for most of their life until this time.

CASE EXAMPLE: JACK

Jack changed his name unofficially in January. He changed his name on social media and told his friends and work colleagues. Jack had known he was Jack for some time and was keen to change his name officially but decided to wait for a few months to change it legally to make sure his name was 'right'. Jack had a very positive response to his name change – both from friends and for himself – so he decided to change it legally sooner than he had initially anticipated. The process of changing his name was quite onerous and bureaucratic, but well worth it.

CASE EXAMPLE: WILL

Will developed the awareness of his gender being different to that assigned him at birth over quite a short period of time, just a matter of months. Will, being assigned female at birth and given a female name, had separately and secretly lived with an awareness of discomfort with his assigned birth name, so called himself a name associated with being male but hadn't actually clocked he was male and not female. In later life, when he became aware he was actually male and not female, he changed his name to reflect the 'Will' he had adopted secretly. Although Will hadn't changed his physical appearance or hormones he was being guided by, he wanted to have his hair cut to begin this process of change. Will therefore chose to go to a barber's shop for his haircut. After all, going to a hairdresser who cut women's hair now seemed wrong (he had always felt uncomfortable in a women's hairdressers but never known why, until his recognition of being transgender). In the shop, the barber said, 'This is a barber's shop, men only.' 'Good,' said Will. 'I'm a man.' For Will, who now always has a 'number 3' to reference the type and shortness of his haircut, this was very affirming and his first public 'outing' of his affirmed name and gender.

Bathrooms

We have always felt uncomfortable with the word 'bathroom' when it is used to refer to toilets because usually the bathroom (public toilets) doesn't have an actually bath in it! However, public toilets (bathrooms) are something of a political issue in the present day. Toilets can be a huge barrier to inclusion for trans and gender-diverse people as other people using the facilities can be hostile. For some people this hostility – perceived or real – stops them from going to the bathroom at all. This limits their ability to do things others take for granted such as going to work or university. You have a right to use the bathroom which aligns with your gender but it is sometimes very difficult to exercise this right. When organizations state their support for people to use whichever bathroom they choose, it makes a huge difference and validates transgender people.

CASE EXAMPLE: MEL

Mel always felt uncomfortable using the public conveniences that appeared to suit their gender – the assigned gender given at their birth. It was the same feeling they experienced when shopping for underwear in large shops. Mel expected others in the store or conveniences to say, 'What are you doing here? You are in the wrong place. The men's toilet is next door.' Then, after Mel's transition process had begun and they decided they were more comfortable in the conveniences for males, they began using these conveniences instead of those for 'ladies'. At first, Mel found it difficult to cope with the 'smells' and the different layout. Over time, however, they adjusted and became more used to these differences. Mel found ways to cope, such as sucking mints, when they used these facilities, which helped to mask some of the discomforts.

66 {YENN} We may feel uncomfortable using the gendered bathrooms at work and in public. When I used the 'female' bathroom it never felt right. The accessible bathroom at my workplace doubles as the shower. There was a sign stuck on the door saying 'Disabled people only to use this facility'. I really wanted to use the accessible bathroom as it also said 'unisex', but I was put off by the sign. I mentioned this issue to my manager and she immediately made a sign for the door which said 'For people who need to use this facility', which includes me. Now I go to the accessible bathroom and I feel so good about it. I find it more difficult to use the unisex/

accessible bathroom in public places like airports as I worry about people questioning my right to be there, but the situation at work is excellent. "

Physical and social changes

Physical changes (superficial and deep) occur as one's body takes on a different appearance due to changes in hairstyles, clothing, hormones and possible surgical interventions.

Social changes occur when individuals change how they socialize (who they mix with), where they socialize (different clubs, meetings they engage with) and what activities they engage with, which are different to those before their transition. To transition socially doesn't require any medical intervention, although some individuals choose to do both (make social and medical changes). These changes may mean changes in dress code, ways of sitting (not crossing their legs/ crossing their legs), hairstyle and general body image, as well as in how our voice sounds (we may practise speaking at a higher pitch, etc.).

Medical intervention

With regard to gender, this is when we engage with any action that causes biological changes to our body. Usually individuals assigned female at birth predominantly have oestrogen as the guiding hormone giving rise to female reproductive characteristics (rounded hips, smooth facial skin, breasts and vagina, less muscle mass generally than in males and usually the capacity to produce ova). In males, body shape shows squarer hips, wider shoulders, a penis and testicles, facial hair, a deeper voice and the ability to produce semen, which are all governed by the hormone testosterone.

In most countries, the age a person is allowed to access gender-affirmation surgery is 18 years. The decision to have surgery needs to be made in consultation with a qualified medical professional. Hormones can generally be prescribed at the age of 16. Some children take puberty blockers at a younger age. Once again, this needs to be done in consultation with a qualified medical practitioner.

If we opt for medical intervention we choose to change how our body will look, possibly sound and also impact its function. For example, a biological female whose body has operated with female hormones but who wishes to medically transition into the male gender and male form, and who has capacity to reproduce, may wish to have their eggs harvested before the surgical removal of their uterus. This allows an individual to choose, down the track, an 'artificial' way for human reproduction allowing for the possibility of children via artificial insemination using a sperm donor and surrogate mother.

Although taking testosterone changes the voice box leading to a masculine voice (within three months), ceasing testosterone and taking oestrogen doesn't reverse this or give a female-sounding voice.

Trans women have to work harder at achieving a female-sounding voice. For them, this might mean going for voice training or coaching.

Fertility and reproduction

Having breasts removed and a male chest sculpted gives the look of masculinity but won't initially change the ability to reproduce, unless the uterus is removed. Some trans guys choose to keep their vagina, uterus and ovaries. If you choose to take testosterone (via gel or injection), however, it will impact this ability to reproduce but not necessarily prevent it. Usually, after a matter of weeks on testosterone, the ability to menstruate ceases. But, again, a word of caution as some trans guys have been known to get pregnant because they believed testosterone prevented this. Of course, over time it will. If you choose to cease testosterone, although some changes revert back to how it was, many will remain (deeper voice, facial hair). If you choose surgical assignment to help towards gender affirmation, and all the reproductive elements of the gender you are moving away from are removed, they are gone permanently, along with any hope of reproduction naturally. If you are young enough and female, you can choose to 'freeze' your eggs and these will be kept for you. If you decide to use them and have children by another, this is very possible. If you are male and transitioning to female and your reproductive ability is removed, you also may choose to freeze your sperm before having the surgery. The process to freeze your sperm can be costly and not available to everyone.

In this chapter, we have written much about gender, gender identity and gender transition. We probably haven't answered every question you have, but there is still more information throughout the book in the other chapters. However, we hope we have answered most and also offered direction so you can check out further those questions you still have.

CHAPTER 3

Coming Out

Introduction

Coming out – what to expect and how to manage it – can be a very tricky and highly personalized process. If you have been 'hiding' from the world due to your autism and have found the whole social world overwhelming, coming out to others might be very uncomfortable. However, if you are more at home with being upright, forthright and know your rights, you might travel through life not noting the impact you have on the lives of others. Whoever you are and whatever your disposition, this journey will be fraught with obstacles that you might not have thought of or previously encountered. If facing the world in the form you had before transitioning was hard, for some of you, being in the gender that's right for you can make things easier. However, it takes time and courage as well as discrimination to work out all those intricate details of what's right for you, who to tell, when to tell and even when not to tell. This chapter explores these in more detail.

There is a process of 'coming out' and it needs to happen in stages. In general, those stages will include:

∞ Discovery

∞ Acceptance

∞ Integration

∞ Peer support.

However, the above stages are not clear cut and you might find yourself revisiting these, even after you think you have finished with one or all of them.

❝ {WENN} I thought I had fully integrated my trans self into my psyche and into my everyday life. It took six years, however, to appreciate that there are often new people, new places and new events that have elements to them of my past and things keep popping up that still had that flavour and needed me to build over them or onto them, depending on the event. ❞

The term 'coming out' refers to being public about your gender identity. It's important to own who you are to yourself and, sometimes, to others. But equally, sometimes it's important not to be public about your gender identity. This can be because it's not necessary, not appropriate, not safe or not comfortable for you to do so.

Coming out to others is often influenced by how we feel about ourselves. Sometimes, at the beginning of our journey, we may feel somehow caught in the middle, not quite who we once were and not yet who we are hoping to be. This can mean we may feel 'silly' or lacking in confidence to say we are transgender or we are gender questioning, because to others we may appear much the same as the person they thought they knew. They may not see 'things' through our eyes. Don't be put off by this, because the person you are becoming takes time to emerge, much like a butterfly who takes time to shed its outer coat before drying off, spreading those wings and leaving that empty chrysalis behind.

Having said this though, we need to remember, just like that butterfly takes their core self with them, so do we. Our overcoat (outer appearance) may change, but the core of who we each are stays the same. By this we mean, the essential 'us' hasn't changed. It may take time for us to connect the dots to the person we are developing into, and, due to possible hormonal changes, we might not feel like 'us' some days, but this process isn't changing the core of who we are, just helping us grow into more of our complete selves. Being patient with ourselves is a useful part of this process.

" {WENN} I still have photographs of my 'former' image above the mantle in our living room. Taking these away will happen for me in time but I've found it hard to let them go. It's almost like if I remove them I'm taking away the memory of those precious times too! I only want images of the person I've become decorating our home, but because I transitioned late in life, all those times with our family, grandchildren and pets would need to come down. It will be easier to swap the pictures over, once the grandkids get older and the pictures of us together represent us from now on. That time is fast approaching! Of course, what works for me will be different from what works for you. "

The theme here is, 'What works?' It's okay to take your time to work out what you need to do that is the most comfortable for you.

Family can mean the people and home you were born into, adopted into or attached yourself to. At times, it's the hardest thing to share yourself with this group. This is the group who may have the biggest influence over us, or the group we want to have acceptance from, or the group we don't want to upset! However, we are not doing ourselves, or them, any great favour by pretending to be someone we are not. It might mean we need to pick our moment, a moment when we and they are happy and not stressed by other things, but we do need to tell them. If you have some information and stories from others who might be well-known figures, this may be helpful because family can see that we can be okay too. Often family fear what they don't understand. They only know the 'us' we have given them access to previously. So, the changes we are proposing, whether a name change, pronoun change, gender change and so on, may come as a shock. Of course, some families will have already worked out what might be happening for us before we do! Either way though, change – any change – will take some time for us to get used to.

Friends are usually those individuals we trust and feel safe with. Friends can be very supportive, or they may be quite the opposite.

❝ {WENN} I found some of those I thought were close friends became the very people who were the most upset with me. I always hoped my friends would value me for 'me' whatever my gender or sexual orientation. But, friends are people too and they have all sorts of baggage with them. For example, one friend said to me, 'Are you doing this for male privilege?' This friend was a person who found the patriarchal society we live in very offensive, quite rightly too, but she passed on her fears and assumptions to what I was telling her about me. I don't think this was intentional, but it hurt. 99

So, again, we need to be prepared for a variety of reactions to news that, for us, is precious. We do not want our discoveries, which may be exciting, tenuous, fearful and so on, to be trashed by others. We need to tread carefully and our aim is to build a collective understanding and accepting community of others who will take the journey with us, rather than try to disrupt and/or destroy our hopes and dreams.

Colleagues and work mates are often people we spend lots of time with but may not be people who know us intimately, and there is usually no need for them to. If they happen to be friends as well as colleagues, this might be different and quite uncomfortable. It's important to weigh up what your priorities are and separate these, if you can. For example, does this person need to know? What difference will it make if I share with them about my gender transition? Mostly, when at work, our gender will not change our working situation. If there are objections to you choosing which 'bathroom' you are most comfortable using, then you might need to discuss this with an appropriate person. Otherwise, it might not be necessary for you to come out to your colleagues.

Teachers and other education personnel might need to be informed of your transition. Again, it might be a decision based on 'who needs to know?' Some schools are really great at accommodating their trans students, others are not. There is quite a bit of material out there now, in the public and education sector, to help schools and places of higher education keep up to date with issues relating to gender. For our trans population who are autistic, this can be less so. Having a supportive teacher at college can make all the difference to whether or not you feel okay. It's wonderful to be understood and to have the appropriate accommodations in place for you. Inclusion isn't just about being in the same place as others, it's about being treated with the same respect – that is every person's right – as anyone else.

Health professionals and other medical staff might need to know your gender status, but again this only applies to those medics who personally treat you.

❝ {WENN} I wear a bracelet that has medical emergency information (allergies) available for those who might need it. I remember going into hospital and not being able to access language or movement (i.e. I couldn't move and I couldn't talk). I couldn't use the bathroom or instruct others about my gender-affirming surgeries and I was terrified they might use a regular size catheter on me to enable me to pass urine. This could have meant such a procedure would have damaged me! I needed them to know they should use the smaller size catheter, one used on a child. Fortunately for me, my wife was able to tell the team what my needs were. These days I carry a letter around with me, just in case of emergencies. It has all my medication and other medical needs written down. This means others, who may need to know if I'm in some form of medical emergency, can read what it is I need from them. ❞

Family of choice might seem like a contradiction but your 'chosen' family consists of those who accept you for who you are and they want the best for you. They support you in your chosen ventures, help you when you need to make decisions and tell you when you might be going down the wrong track! As in any other family, you might have your differences, but they are always there for you. If you can find yourself among a unit of supporters who love you unconditionally, will offer a place to you that allows you to be yourself, safely and without barriers, you might have found your 'chosen' family. This family might not be all in one place.

{WENN} My family are spread out across the globe and we connect as and when we do. I can always ring them, text or email, if I can't catch up in person.

What if I am 'not trans enough'?

Many of us want very much to 'pass' in our trans identity. We think we are not really 'trans' or 'trans enough' unless others only recognize us in our trans identity rather than in the gender we were assigned at birth. We feel our gender identity does not always match the 'image' we have of how we should look to earn the right or claim to that label. We simply feel 'not trans enough'.

{YENN} I was involved in an event for International Women's Day about 12 months after I came out as non-binary. The organization putting on the event was inclusive of trans and gender-diverse people and invited me to be involved as a non-binary person. However, when I posted pictures of the event on social media, someone criticized me for being involved in a women's day event and basically implied that I was not really non-binary if I chose to be part of this event, despite the fact that the chair of the organization hosting it is also non-binary. I was filled with self-doubt in response to the comments and had to consciously tell myself that the person making the comments was the one in the wrong and not me. Identity can be such a fragile thing. 〞

Gender identity is representative of our true nature and is not reflected by our bodily look. Some of us don't feel trans enough because we didn't recognize our gender when we were younger or we are not very tall/too tall or we don't have a very masculine/feminine voice and so on. If we are trans, we are trans!

〝 {WENN} I've spent such a lot of time looking at cis guys and then comparing them to me. It's interesting really because, at the very least, I came to realize that many males have bigger 'butts' than I had believed, are often not as tall in general, are not always muscular in build and their beards are not tidy and well crafted!

Being transgender is not about being or fitting the societal stereotype for that gender. Being trans is about 'feeling' at home with a particular 'gender(s)' identity while being at home with yourself. I'm a trans guy aged 68 and I love soft toys, cats, singing and some romantic novels (as well as science fiction, books and TV shows). I don't like drinking beer in a pub, loud music, fighting, sport or violent video games. I've given birth to four children who still call me 'Mum', but I'm a 'man mum' who loves being a parent and grandparent and I'm very proud of who I am. 〞

So, the message is clear, we can be trans while being ourselves, and that might mean not fitting the 'gender role' traditionally expected by others. It might even mean our own beliefs and our own biases need challenging too. You can watch some others sharing their concepts about being 'trans enough' on YouTube.[1]

It's very 'usual' to not feel 'trans enough' and it's also part of our journey towards 'feeling' trans. It takes time to change our emotional concepts of who we are today from who we were in our past (not just our body differences either).

Coming out to self

It can be very uncomfortable to know what 'coming out to yourself' might mean. Again, this is different for each of us. Sometimes joining a support group, in person or online, can be very helpful. It's about chatting with others and listening to one another's 'story'. This process can help us identify our own needs and we can also form some friendships with others that help support our own journey.

❝ {YENN} I found a support group online and it's a place where I can be myself and share with others who know exactly what I mean and what I'm going through. The group 'Autistic and trans' comes from all over the world and members chat together about whether or not to bind their chest, where to find the best aids to support them with physically 'passing' in a public bathroom and so on. The trans females share information about voice coaching, make-up and fashion as well as the

---

1   www.youtube.com/watch?v=_7LNk0QHJtw; www.youtube.com/watch?v=NGo8gL64SNQ

best ways to deal with hair removal and wearing wigs. There's talk about experiences with the medical profession as well as ideas of coming out to family, friends and colleagues. "

" {WENN} Coming out to myself was not a long process for me because I knew in an instant what I needed to do. It was more about a daily renewing of my understanding and a positive statement or acclamation of confidence in my decision. I never once doubted my decision to transition but, when I looked into a mirror, I didn't see a man looking back at me. So, I needed to affirm to myself that the outer physical image that looked back at me was simply housing the man I was and this would change as I progressed through my transition process. "

Now this might not be your experience. You might be an individual who has decided not to take hormones or change your outward appearance. This is absolutely fine! Whatever way you need to affirm your transition – socially, medically or both – it is up to you. It might be words you speak, clothes you wear, music you listen to, pictures you draw – whatever it is, it's your way of being 'out' to yourself and it's important.

Being public and out requires lots of courage and you might not be totally ready for this yet. It's vital you go at a pace that suits you and you don't push yourself too hard. There is no right or wrong way to do this, but if you feel you got it wrong, don't knock yourself, simply accept that this is part of the process. Knowing when, where and how takes practice and we won't always get it right the first time. This will mean that sometimes we venture out as our 'trans' self and at other times we don't.

66 {YENN} I found that as I 'practised' being publicly 'out' I became more and more confident and at home. 99

It's important to keep yourself safe and only do this when you are sure you will be. If you need to go out in the company of friends, do this. Don't push yourself beyond your comfort zone. You are not letting yourself down in any way, you are being sensible and reasonable. Remember, 'coming out' and 'being out' take time.

The above journey is different for everyone and this must be stressed. As autistic individuals with so many different life experiences, family and cultural differences as well as personality differences, we can only benefit from being patient with ourselves and taking the time we need to mature into the person we are happiest being.

Intimate relationships

Intimate relationships can mean different things for different people. For some, this represents a romantic and/or physical relationship, including sexual intimacy. For others, it's about an 'intimate' friendship that allows people to share intimate personal experiences together, but it might not be a physical or romantic relationship. Intimacy is all about feeling safe and welcomed by another to mutually share personal things. It's important that we only intimately share our personal lives with those whom it is safe to do so. Finding out if a person is a safe person to do this with isn't always easy.

Qualities of a trustworthy person include their reputation; is it a good one that implies they have a trustworthy personality and know how to keep private information to themselves? Are they available to you and are they willing to relate to you in ways you need them to? Although it is important to be upfront with issues related to our autism, sometimes non-autistic people find it hard to understand our sensory and cognitive challenges, so we need to be sure they are comfortable discussing these and that they appreciate the depth of how our autism impacts us.

Being honest and upfront with any intimate partner, whom we trust and wish to pursue a relationship with, is paramount to success. They need to know our gender and they need to be happy with us. If coming out to a partner who has only known us in our previous gender is a concern for you, it really is imperative you get the timing right. Don't try and tell them you think you are in the wrong body when you have argued over something, when they are unwell or if they are in a bad mood, tired or have had a rough day. Let them know you have some important news to share with them (when the timing is right and they appear relaxed) and make sure you affirm your commitment to the relationship. Once you have shared your news you need to allow them time to process this and you need to be prepared that they might not want to still be in a relationship. After all, they thought they were getting a person of the gender you introduced yourself in, and this might be the only gender they are attracted to.

66 {WENN} A friend of mine said to me that when she asked her husband how he would feel if she were to become a man he replied, 'I'd be okay as long as you kept your vagina!' She was a bit surprised by this as she knew if her husband became a woman, it wouldn't faze her.

In my own experience with my wife, my coming out to her

was very dramatic. Sometimes I think we survived it because we are both autistic and in love with the person, not their gender. We were very co-dependent on one another and I looked to her for reassurance that I was getting it right or I was doing the right thing. After my transition, however, the co-dependent nature of our relationship changed. I think testosterone gave me a sense of autonomy I had previously lacked. So, for me the change was great, but for her it added more layers of trauma. 🙶

Co-dependency

🙶 {WENN} Because I wasn't connected to understanding what I felt or what I needed (largely due to poor interoception[2] and poor self-confidence), I depended on others to know for me. Throughout childhood I rarely noticed others – how they looked, what they wore, and what they expected from me. I did my own thing, whatever came to mind usually, and often inappropriately. This got me into lots of trouble! As a way to avoid trouble I became a shadow to whoever the significant other was in my life at the time and became very co-dependent (Lawson & Lawson, 2017). I found making my own decisions intolerable, all of the time. It was as if I couldn't trust myself to get it right. Some of these things changed dramatically after I transitioned from female to male (Lawson & Lawson, 2017). Maybe having testosterone (the right hormone for me) coursing through my body helped connect my senses. Maybe due to being more confident (because I was joined up) I attempted

---

2   Interoception (our eighth sense) is the term describing our inner awareness of bodily senses such as breathing, heart rate, hunger, thirst and temperature

more things on my own, which led to needing to depend on others less.

I know my interoceptive sense still needs working on, but being at home with who I am has given me a good start. It might be this is true for you and that coming out to your partner is full of anxiety because you worry about their response and can't imagine life without them. I can only encourage you to ask yourself the question: 'If it's truth that sets us free, what is my truth?' If being trans is your truth you will never be free until you own it. If you are prepared to live your life being untruthful to yourself and others, or only living a half-life, this is your decision to make. I wish I could release you from the discomfort this carries, but I know I cannot. My partner surprised me and, although it's been traumatic with loads of stuff to work through, she has been there all the way. 〞

Being trans doesn't make you a lesser person, you never need to apologize for who you are. Sometimes others around you will forget to use the right pronoun or will forget your name and call you by some term that no longer defines you. It's usually okay to gently remind them; at other times, you might let it go. But you need never take any notice of the discomfort you feel, at least not if it makes you feel bad, because it will change. This situation is part of the process we all go through and we benefit by being patient with ourselves.

For some of us, coming out might be a process that only happens for ourselves, a kind of internal knowing. This is fine, we do not need to tell anyone else if this is how we feel and this is the most comfortable way for us.

〝 {WENN} There certainly was a time when an understanding of who I am grew within me and I was unsure of whether or not to express it. Over time, I decided I would share my thoughts and awareness with trusted others. This was more a part of the process of discovering and testing my growing awareness with others, so I could check it out. I still do this at times, but the need has decreased over time. "

" {YENN} Coming out for me was a gradual process. I didn't have the language for my non-binary identity for most of my life. It simply didn't exist. I always felt uncomfortable with being female and felt like I was some kind of third option but nobody had articulated any option which fitted me. I knew about the transgender experience through some trans friends but I didn't want to be a man. When I learned about non-binary I thought it described me better than anything else had but I still wasn't confident to come out. I spent about two years testing out whether I was non-binary, so it had been in my thinking for a while. When I came out, it happened fairly seamlessly, mostly because I had been working out if that was 'me' for a while. "

Coming out to yourself is the first step in feeling and building a foundation in your mind and heart of your true self. It's possible this is all you need. Coming out to yourself gives you the opportunity to safely explore who you want to be. You can try things on (a new name, an outfit, doing your nails, a hairstyle, going to a club with a mate to observe), discard them, try something else and so on. If you choose to 'come out' to others, remember it takes time for those others to get used to your new pronouns and new name. It's okay to ask someone what their *name* and *pronouns* are (i.e. she/her, he/him, they/

them) but it's not okay to ask about a person's transition, surgery, body or history – this is private information you/they have to volunteer your/themselves. You can only control your responses towards yourself and others. You cannot control what others may say or do. However, you can lead by example and you can inform others of what you need from them.

CHAPTER 4

Work and College

Introduction

This chapter attempts to outline some of the hurdles and challenges being autistic and trans might present at your place of work and education. Places of employment and study are not allowed to discriminate against an employee or student on grounds of race, gender, disability or sexuality. However, not all employees or students declare these areas of their lives because it isn't necessary or because they consider it not in their best interests. Sometimes it's difficult to judge whether or not you need to share this information. It's hoped this chapter will assist with this decision, at least in the area of gender.

Work

Many trans and gender-diverse autistic people work. It is an important part of life and gives us a range of intangible benefits in addition to an income, or it should at least. However, for many trans and gender-diverse people and particularly trans and gender-diverse autistic people, the world of work can be less than welcoming. This chapter includes some practical help and information around being trans and autistic in the workplace, including some sample transitioning guidelines which provide guidance on how workplaces and managers can support people who are affirming their gender.

Finding work

When you are trans and autistic it can seem almost impossible to find a job, and many people take jobs which aren't suited to their skills and interests in order to earn an income. Employment service providers can be ill-equipped to support a job search for trans and autistic people and some face bigotry from these agencies when trying to find a job. Society needs to change a lot in this space, as not only is the high unemployment rate for trans and gender-diverse autistic people a sign of the bigotry and discrimination which exists, it also represents a waste of talent. Autistic people often bring some high-level skills to the workplace, and denying them access to work is often to the detriment of employers. Despite this being the case, many employers have not quite caught up in this regard.

There are some employment programmes and workplaces which only employ autistic people but these are not everywhere and do not suit everyone. However, it may be worth seeking out an opportunity with one of these programmes if they are in your area as they are tailored to autistic people and usually offer well-paid and secure work. It should be noted that these programmes are not always free from transphobia. Some agencies to consider, if they are in your locality, are:

∞ Specialisterne Foundation[1]

∞ ASPECT[2]

∞ Autism and Agriculture.[3]

For other support see the Ambitious About Autism website.[4]

Many autistic people who are also transgender find work in areas related to their experience such as in advocacy or representation roles or as academics and researchers. There are some autism specialist employment service providers and employment agencies which have a greater understanding of the needs of autistic people and there are LGBTQIA+ employment agencies in some countries as well. These may be more suited to your needs than generalist recruitment services if you are looking for work.

❝ {WENN} Recently I was talking with a friend who felt 'very out of it', and when I asked her if there was any specific contributing factor she said she thought it was mostly because she didn't fit the typical idea of autism. She is an actress and loves theatre. In some of the textbooks on autism it says autistic people are not very imaginative and lack insight into themselves and others. Well, this might be true for some but certainly not true for others. I'm reminded that it's not useful to compare myself to the lives of others and even the textbooks

---

1   http://specialisternefoundation.com
2   www.autismspectrum.org.au/how-can-we-help/getting-a-job
3   www.autismcrc.com.au/sites/default/files/inline-files/3_Robert%20van%20
     Barneveld_SunPork%20Group.pdf
4   www.ambitiousaboutautism.org.uk/sites/default/files/resources-and-downloads/
     files/autism-in-the-workplace-report.pdf

can get it wrong! Being oneself is as complicated as we make it at times – we have a tendency to overthink things. Taking a step back and another deep breath may help. Also, reading stories of others who are autistic and trans is very useful too, because we realize that autistic people are everywhere, in every profession and are all so different. One of the problems with textbooks is that they quickly become outdated and most, on autism, have been written by non-autistic people! 〟

Disclosure – gender and autism

Disclosure is a word used to describe telling others about a part of your identity and experience, for example autism or gender diversity. In the workplace, being autistic and being trans can result in stigma but also in support and respect, depending on the workplace and your colleagues and managers.

The decision to disclose or not can be a really difficult one and there are pros and cons for both disclosing and not disclosing. If you transition or affirm gender while in the same job there can be a disclosure of your gender identity by default, especially if you make changes to your gender expression, pronouns and name. Autism can be easier to keep to yourself but it is often not helpful to do so. Being out as autistic can mean you are able to obtain workplace adjustments – such as those to help accommodate sensory issues – and can mean your team understands you better. People tend to see others through the lens of their own experience, which means managers and colleagues who do not know you are autistic may view you as if you are neurotypical/allistic.[5] This often results in judgement and censure. However, if they know you

---

5   Allistic is a term used to describe the population who are not autistic

are autistic and (importantly) understand what that means for you, then your life at work may be easier.

All workplaces are different, so it may be easier to be an 'out' autistic and trans person in one workplace rather than another. You can get something of a feel of how supportive and inclusive your employer is through the emphasis they place on diversity and inclusion. For example, if they celebrate Wear it Purple Day or International Day for People with Disability and promote those events to staff, the chances are it will be a more inclusive place to work. It is important to note that inclusive workplaces may have bigoted individuals working in them. However, it is also true that unsupportive workplaces may have allies and supporters working in them.

You may be the only 'out' autistic and trans person in your workplace, which can feel like a big responsibility! However, you shouldn't be expected to educate everyone at your workplace if you don't want to, and the fact you exist does not mean you have to become an advocate or activist if you do not wish to. It can be helpful to participate in your workplace's disability staff network or Pride or LGBTQIA+ network if they have one, as these are places to find like-minded people at work. Membership of these kinds of networks can make work a little bit less daunting for trans and gender-diverse autistic people, because you are not alone.

Elements of work

Some elements of work can be very challenging for trans and gender-diverse autistic people. Things like answering phone calls can be doubly challenging – many autistic people dislike phone conversations anyway. Phone calls can in addition be fraught as someone's voice might not tally with the gendered expectation of the caller. Sadly, not all callers are respectful or accepting, making phone calls a bit of a minefield. Customer-facing work can also pose a challenge and people can be subjected to transphobic and ableist discrimination. Challenging a customer or calling them out on their poor behaviour is often not acceptable to management and could lead to the employee being disciplined or losing their job. Colleagues and managers can be disrespectful and discriminatory, sometimes without even consciously recognizing that they are. Human Resources systems (payroll, etc.) often do not have the option of selecting gender X or of non-gendered titles (e.g. Mx), leaving trans and gender-diverse employees who use those with no way to accurately and appropriately record their title and gender status.

Some employees will elect to leave their job prior to transition and find another job as their affirmed gender. For autistic people, this can be particularly challenging given how hard it is to find work as an autistic person.

Workplace transitioning guidelines

Some employers have transitioning guidelines to support employees transitioning/affirming gender. The information in these sorts of guidelines can inform your understanding of transitioning at work. It is good practice for employers to provide advice to managers and employees about gender affirmation at work. Some sample guidelines for a corporate workplace outlining what should be expected from employers, managers and colleagues in relation to a person's gender affirmation/transition can be found below.

SAMPLE TRANSITIONING/ GENDER-AFFIRMATION GUIDELINES

About the guidelines

These transitioning guidelines outline the company's approach to supporting employees who transition gender, including requirements for managers and colleagues.

Publicly changing your gender presentation in society is known as 'transitioning' or 'affirming gender'.

Transitioning can be a significant process and can impact almost every part of a person's life. Everyone who transitions will have their own set of unique circumstances and preferences. Transitions can have psychological, physiological and social components that may take place over an extended period of time.

The person transitioning often legally changes their name as well as their clothing and appearance to coincide with their gender identity. Some will make physical changes such as hormone replacement therapy, surgery, and/or other actions to support affirmation of gender.

As with any significant life event, employees who are transitioning may benefit from additional support. It is also important for the individual to work with their manager to allow for a smooth transitioning process in the workplace.

Transitioning can be a positive and liberating experience, but it can also trigger difficult situations and interactions in a person's personal, professional and family lives.

There is no single formula for managing transitions

in the workplace well but these guidelines aim to facilitate an inclusive and supportive process of transition for employees transitioning and their managers and colleagues.

About gender diversity and identity

The term 'transgender' is commonly used to describe anyone whose gender identity does not align with the gender recorded on their birth certificate. Gender identity refers to a person's deeply held, internal sense of who they are.

A person classified as female at birth who identifies as a man may describe themselves as trans, a trans man or a man. Similarly, a person classified as male at birth who identifies as a woman may use the label trans, a trans woman or a woman. Some people identify as non-binary gender, which means they do not identify as entirely male or female. Some people choose not to use any of these descriptions.

Sexuality is not a factor that necessarily determines or relates to gender identity. The sexuality of transgender people can include being gay, lesbian, bisexual, pansexual, asexual or heterosexual, or some people may use another term or choose not to categorize their sexuality.

It is important to understand that the gender a person identifies with is their true gender (regardless of their birth record) and must be respected.

The discrimination or harassment of a person because they are transitioning gender is unlawful discrimination. Managers must communicate and model acceptable behaviour. Transphobic[6] behaviour is not tolerated at [the company].

Managers should communicate and model appropriate and respectful behaviour. Discrimination will be dealt with in the same way as any other unacceptable behaviour.

Workplace etiquette

Employees who are transitioning are entitled to be treated with respect by their managers and colleagues and all other employees. Transgender people experience discrimination at high rates. This is something which should never happen. Colleagues and managers have the capacity and responsibility to ensure discrimination does not happen in the workplace.

Bathroom and change rooms

Transgender employees are entitled to use the bathroom of their affirmed gender. There is signage in company bathrooms affirming the right of employees to use their preference of bathroom without harassment or questioning their right to be there.

---

6   Transphobia is a term that is used to describe negative attitudes and bigotry against trans and gender-diverse individuals

Names and pronouns

An employee transitioning has the right to be addressed by the name and pronouns that they want to be called. If it is not clear which pronouns to use, it is appropriate to respectfully ask which name and pronouns to use.

Once a transgender person presents in the workplace in their affirmed gender it is important that they are referred to using their affirmed name and pronouns. It is highly disrespectful and hurtful to refer to a transgender person by the name they used before they transitioned (their 'dead name'). However, it is quite common for people to accidentally misgender[7] someone if they knew them before they transitioned. If this occurs, a simple, genuine apology is appropriate.

Addressing workplace or education harassment

Transgender staff and/or students may be particularly vulnerable to harassment and discrimination. Managers and education leaders must take reasonable steps to prevent staff and students from being harassed, bullied and discriminated against by colleagues or others. Deliberate misgendering is not acceptable behaviour.

People who are from their place of education or from their employer need to:

---

7   Misgendering means describing or addressing someone using language that does not match a person's gender identity

- feel safe

- feel supported

- feel able to raise concerns with their manager

- be treated with courtesy and respect.

Updating records

There are a number of things to consider when an employee transitions in relation to records and administrative systems. These include:

- updating the email signature block

- updating details, which may include diversity details in the company's Human Resources records system

- organizing to have a new photo to be placed on their security pass if they wish.

Transitioning employees may also need to update tax records, update bank accounts, inform their superannuation and/or insurance provider(s) of their name and gender change, and so on.

For managers of transitioning employees

When an employee approaches their manager and states their intention to transition, it is important for the manager to be supportive, open-minded and honest.

Managers should be prepared to discuss the transitioning employee's aims and expectations and confirm what they want the manager's role to be.

Managers should consider stakeholders, colleagues, policies and procedures existing in the workplace and contact the Human Resources Diversity and Inclusion team for guidance and support as needed.

The responsibilities of a manager assisting a transitioning employee will vary depending on the situation and the preferences of the individual. However, they could include:

- working with the transitioning employee to understand their goals and discuss related matters, including the development of a transition plan

- developing a shared understanding about agreed work arrangements during the workplace transition period

- protecting the privacy of the transitioning employee and maintaining confidentiality

- being flexible and supportive of any leave that may be required by the transitioning employee

- setting expectation of respectful behaviour with the transitioning employee's colleagues

- increasing their own level of understanding on gender diversity by seeking resources and education if required

- providing leadership to develop a positive, inclusive and respectful environment to support a successful transition.

Managers are largely responsible for ensuring that the transitioning employee is safe and that the workplace is respectful. Empathy is important.

For employees who are transitioning

Planning a conversation with your manager where you express that you are transitioning can be helpful. Things to consider include:

- Who are you going to tell?

- What are you going to tell them?

- Are you happy for them to tell others (e.g. your colleagues)?

- If so, what do you want them to say to your colleagues or would you prefer to talk to your colleagues yourself?

- Are there things you need from your manager?

You can request support from the company's LGBTQIA+/Pride network in relation to coming out, including having a representative of the network sit in on the conversation.

What do you do if you experience bigotry at work?

First, be aware that bigotry and bullying are not in any way your fault. They are the fault and responsibility of the bigot or bully.

[The company] does not condone bullying or discrimination and takes it very seriously.

There are a number of avenues for addressing bullying and/or discrimination, including making a complaint to your manager or making a formal complaint to Human Resources.

Making a complaint can be difficult and bring up additional traumatic memories. There is no legal requirement to report bullying and it is often preferable to trying to manage it yourself.

It is possible that you will receive questions from colleagues about your transition. It is not your responsibility to educate others or do any advocacy around transgender rights and experience unless you wish to.

Probing questions can be a form of harassment.

Work tasks

Some work tasks can be challenging for transgender people such as taking calls from the public. If you have any concerns about your work tasks, inform your manager and discuss how to accommodate your needs.

Terminology

Terminology	Definition
Affirmed gender	The gender you identify with. This may or may not match your gender at birth.
Ally	An ally is a supporter or advocate for the LGBTQIA+ community. Being an ally is about using inclusive language, showing respect and support for LGBTQIA+ people through your actions and your words. Allies to lesbian, gay and bisexual people are generally straight, and allies to transgender people are generally cisgender.
Cisgender	People whose gender identity aligns with their assigned sex at birth. It is an appropriate term for people who are not transgender.
Coming out	The process of recognizing and acknowledging (to yourself and to others) your sexuality or gender identity.
Family	Family may mean biological family or family of choice. Some LGBTQIA+ people may form close relationship links with others who they may refer to as their 'family of choice'. Some LGBTQIA+ people are not accepted by their biological family, making their family of choice important to them.
Gender diverse	People whose knowledge and expression of gender does not conform to the social expectations placed on them based on their sex assigned at birth.
Gender identity; gender expression	The identity, appearance or other gender-related characteristics of a person. This includes the way people express their gender.

Terminology	Definition
LGBTQIA+	People with diverse sexual orientation, sex or gender identity. LGBTQIA+ is short for lesbian, gay, bisexual, transgender, queer, intersex, asexual.
Misgendering	Using language that does not match a person's gender identity.
Non-binary gender identity	Someone with a gender identity other than male or female. There is a large range of non-binary gender identities.
Transgender	Transgender (sometimes referred to as 'trans') is a term used to describe a wide range of gender identities that differ from social expectations assigned to biological sex. Transgender can mean people with a gender identity that does not match their birth gender, someone who identifies as both genders, no gender or a third gender.
Transition	Both the public act and the process of affirming gender.
Transphobia	Hatred and discrimination against people who are transgender, or who are thought to be transgender.

Disclosure – gender and autism at work or college

Coming out as trans or gender fluid and so on has been written about in Chapter 3. However, coming out at work or in your place of education is a personal choice.

66 {WENN} I was very happy to begin a particular job where I was only known by my male name and gender and those working with me only 'saw' the 'male' me. However, I chose to share with my close colleagues that I was transgender and it was an experience to have them accept me. But although it brought a kind of relief because I didn't want them to discover my transgender via some other means (social media), it also brought some discomforts. I think the discomfort was around knowing that they now knew who I was and I wondered if they would think of me differently, or negatively. I shared with them my anxiety and it was good to have their feedback. For me, on this occasion, I was told by my female colleagues that they felt my news only made them feel even more comfortable! Although this was lovely to hear, I think it showed my lack of confidence in who I was and where I was in my transition journey. One day, I'll be so at home with who I am, I won't feel that kind of discomfort. We each can only benefit from being kind to ourselves on our transition journey and not giving ourselves a bad time when we have doubts, anxieties and fears. 99

Study

Whether you are a student at school, college or university, there may be times you need or would benefit from sharing your gender journey with another. For example, as autistic individuals, we may need additional support with our studies, and, if this is the case, we may also need extra support due to our transition journey.

    " {WENN} As an autistic trans student with learning difficulty, I needed to let those previously supporting me know of my name and pronoun change. I didn't want to go beyond that though, so I didn't go into personal details (e.g. was I taking hormones; had I had surgery; who was my medical consultant?).

    I often choose to study online rather than physically attend an institution. For me, my autism meant being around lots of busyness and people interfered with my ability to study, so study online worked better. However, even when studying online, I needed to be sure all my details were up to date and each department had access to the right information. This might need to include financial details and all my personal details, such as name, address and date of birth. I remember the excitement I experienced when I received letters addressed to me in my 'right' name and gender. "

Accessing health care

Accessing health care as a trans person can be very tricky. We don't say this to alarm you but it's very important to have medical professionals who support your gender identity and journey. It is your right to access appropriate care but not all medical professionals are equal. Make sure you do your homework and check out the profile of any person you are intending to see. You might even need to phone them or visit in person to check them out.

In some instances, it's not important and you do not need to tell the treating professional your gender identity. You offer up your name, address and date of birth, possibly any medical health number you might need to show, and it ends there. Knowing which professional to tell can be difficult to work out, but often the best way is to ask yourself some questions. For example:

∞ Does telling this professional my gender identity impact on my care needs? If not, then don't.

∞ Does telling this professional my gender identity impact how they care for me? If not, then don't.

∞ Does my gender identity make a difference to how, where or in what way care needs to be delivered to me? If it does, then tell them.

Some medical insurances cover some transgender needs, but not all do. You will need to check with your health insurance agency if necessary, to see what you are covered for.

Renting properties

When we move out of home and explore ways to find our own place we might consider renting an apartment or moving into a shared house with friends, and sometimes with strangers. It's usually our friends who know our gender identity, so this isn't an issue. But, when it comes to sharing with those who may not know us, we need to consider if it's necessary to tell them.

66 {WENN} When I was exploring this for myself as a much older person and was working away from home, I decided not to mention my being transgender and autistic. I couldn't see that this was important for my fellow housemates and they didn't need to know. They were not sharing the bathroom with me, they were not sharing the bedroom with me and my ability to keep the house clean and tidy was not impacted by my gender. 99

However, it is important if you are going to be renting that you have all your references and other paperwork in your preferred name. Your legal name may be used on documentation, and if this is the name that accompanies your gender, all well and good. If it is not, you could be facing some questions that are uncomfortable and could interfere with your renting success. So, aim to have all your paperwork up to date.

Travelling overseas

Overseas travel can be extremely fraught for trans and gender-diverse people and particularly for trans and gender-diverse autistic people. Even if your passport has your affirmed gender, customs officers can be transphobic and question you. There are many examples of autistic trans people being treated badly by customs staff in a number of countries. Some countries have provision for a 'gender X' passport, for use by non-binary and other gender nonconforming people. While this is a great initiative and aims to cover the needs of gender-diverse people, it can result in victimization by border patrol staff in some countries. Some countries are less respectful of trans and gender-diverse people than others, so it may be worth investigating attitudes in countries you wish to visit before you go there. For autistic people, going through customs can be doubly difficult due to the anxiety and sensory issues we live with. Sometimes, when going through customs, it may be easier to travel with a friend or other trusted person.

{YENN} I changed my name in 2019 and wanted to change my passport – both with my correct name but also with gender X, which is an option where I live. The paperwork was immense and I had to provide loads of documentation, including a letter from my psychiatrist. I had the appointment with the psychiatrist and was very anxious as I wasn't sure if he would sign off on it. I figured if he wouldn't, I would get a new psychiatrist, but he was fine and my application was approved. I now have a passport under my correct name with gender X. I wish it wasn't such a process though. Needing a psychiatrist to sign off just seems very pathologizing and, while the current diagnostic literature does not say gender diversity is a mental illness, the passport office evidently thinks it is or I wouldn't have needed a letter from a psychiatrist to officially affirm my gender.

What supports can you access?

Not all countries, governments and local councils have 'in law' the kinds of supports we might need. In some countries and states, it's mandatory to provide community support and mental health advocacy, but if this isn't the case for you, finding appropriate help might be more difficult. Please ask your GP (general practitioner or doctor) for their advice or referral as a place to start. Your GP should be able to direct you to a gender clinic, gender therapist or gender specialist. Sometimes finding a mental health specialist is advised (although gender transition isn't a mental health issue) simply because they can help you navigate your way through the trickiness of your journey.

66 {WENN} When I was transitioning from female to male, I needed a psychiatrist to affirm my gender dysphoria and support my need for further treatment (hormones and surgery). To get to see the psychiatrist, I needed a referral from my GP. It took a long time to get an initial appointment with the psychiatrist because he was a specialist and the only one in my state. Then, when I spent time with him in various appointments, it was soon clear that he found my autism an impediment to accessing a diagnosis. I eventually did get a diagnosis from him, but it took over a year. 99

Usually, for the non-autistic population in particular, it shouldn't take this long! To help speed up the process, it might help if you have supporting documents from your local doctor, other professionals, friends and family, to support your argument (they know and affirm your gender dysphoria), so you hopefully won't need to experience the trauma of a delayed diagnosis.

Advocacy opportunities

Being your own advocate might be easy for you and you might have been advocating for yourself over a long period of time, but if this isn't you then exploring ways to access advocacy will be important. Sometimes being able to take along a friend to the various meetings and appointments you will need to attend can be very helpful. It's unfortunate that this is needed, but sometimes a friend can more readily answer questions and process information more quickly, then translate it back to you afterwards.

66 {WENN} Words are my 'thing', so I often haven't felt the need for an advocate. But the consultant I've gone in to see on reading that I'm autistic has often talked to me in a 'less than equal' way. The person has assumed that being autistic has meant I'm less cognitively able than some and even that my decision-making ability is in question. This is very unsettling and very frustrating, let alone only adding to my anxiety. So, having a person support me in my process of getting initial recognition of my gender dysphoria would have been helpful. 99

Your local LGBTQIA+ community may be able to help you find an advocate who can support you in the process you are going through.

Whether or not you are used to advocating for yourself or if you need an advocate, it's always a good idea to have relevant research and supportive documentation with you. Some people will always argue with you; it's harder to argue with the paperwork though!

CHAPTER 5

Interoception, Camouflaging and Masking

Introduction

This chapter explores ways to look after yourself and stay safe. It also offers tips to look after your mental as well as physical health. It might be you have come late to puberty or you are going through early, not planned for, menopause. Being trans and gender diverse in your place of education might mean being exposed to bullying and this can certainly rob you of your dignity, self-worth and confidence. Building pride and respect can help to protect you, but you need support to do this. Taking on a bully alone can be dangerous, and there is safety in numbers. The value of autistic and trans peers cannot be underestimated, but we also need the support of our typically developing peers and those others who 'get' who we are.

The other issue currently being written about in the literature is 'camouflaging' and 'masking' your autism in order to 'fit in' and be more socially accepted. If masking is something you relate to, this could impact both your gender discovery, your mental health and even your physical health. If we work hard to suppress who we really are, the emotions connected to that energy need to go somewhere. Very often, if these are not expressed externally (via anger and other means), they turn internally and become anxiety and depression. This chapter looks at these issues in more detail and aims to aid you in your own discussions that influence your gender journey.

Being single-minded

As autistic people, we may find it difficult to maintain eye contact, identify emotions of self or others and have difficulties in generalizing concepts. This is the product of single-focused attention, which means we find it difficult to attend to several things happening (from self or other) at the same time. This has often been misinterpreted as poor 'theory of mind' (knowing that how you act, what you talk about and so on is going to impact how other people treat you) or difficulty putting ourselves in another's shoes. But it's actually a matter of attention, so if we notice something we can connect to it.

Object permanence

Object permanence (OP) is the term given to knowing that objects, people, emotions and so on have a life of their own, even when out of sight. Small infants usually gain a sense of OP during their first year of life, but OP is very often delayed in autism. This, of course, has implications for 'noticing' our inner most needs for safety, assurance when things change, and connecting to the various chapters of our lives. For example, when I'm away from 'family' or 'friends' it can 'feel' as if they don't exist. This isn't about not caring or not feeling, it's about a poorer sense of OP!

Interoception

Interoception[1] is known as our eighth sense and it depends on us noticing internal senses rather than reading stimuli from external senses such as sight, hearing and touch. Our inner senses (e.g. temperature, heart rate, hunger) need us to attend and connect to multiple stimuli coming from inside us so that we can self-regulate (understand our emotions and recognize our needs). These also help in differentiating self from other. It's only as we put these all together that we can make sense of the world, our place in it and how to connect safely to others. We would argue gender identity is more about our inner senses, such as our interoception connection. Therefore, having an understanding and being able to connect to our gender will need some attention given to our interoception sense.

Neuroception and interoception: connections with gender identity in autism

Neuroception is the autonomic, unconscious sense that warns the body of danger (Porges, 2004). It allows a person to connect to the five Fs (fight, flight, freeze, flop and fawn). These are the responses we have to perceived and real threats. In

---

1   www.education.sa.gov.au/supporting-students/health-e-safety-and-wellbeing/
     health-support-planning/managing-health-education-and-care/neurodiversity/
     interoception

autism, however, this system will be skewed, meaning we are primed for anxiety and possible hypervigilance, hypovigilance or disconnection. This system works with our interoception. Remember, interoception is a sense like our other senses, but it lets us connect to our internal world (e.g. heart rate, breathing, pain, temperature, appetite, thirst, sexual desire), rather than the external world (e.g. sight, hearing, touch, taste, smell). Interoception is a sense that is often neglected, not just in terms of academic research, but because as human beings we may not realize how important interoception is. We need a good interoceptive sense that is fine-tuned, for example, otherwise we may not have access to self-regulation of our emotions. Without this connection, we will find it difficult to navigate our way through much of our autistic and gender experiences – to separate what is what! We all know about our senses and how difficult it can be to feel connected to the external world, but connection to our inner world and that which helps with connection to identity, and especially gender identity, isn't given much credence. This means it might take us longer to attend to, notice and connect to our feelings so we can work them out. It's important to take time to understand both neuroception and interoception, as these impact on our differing processing systems (which is different to that of the non-autistic population). Therefore, it's doubly important to take time and to explore what remediation is needed to build appropriate connection to our fuller 'selves' that contributes to uncovering the gender identity that is right for us.

So, gender identity in autism isn't just about being a boy, a girl, either, neither or both – it's about connection. Yes, making connection requires attention, a way to notice self and others. Attention in autism tends to be of a singular nature, so we can attend to one thing at a time but not too many at once. It's why we do well with single or focused interests.

However, the way our brain manages attention means we may not notice or connect to the bigger picture. If we come to feel we may be living in the wrong gender identity, we will need help exploring this feeling. This will take time and lots of support from those who love us, walk with us, without judgement, and will go with us all the way. As stated before, for some this will mean social transition only, for others it will mean both social and medical transition – as little or as much as you want, need or can manage.

Some further exploration of this by way of following what others have done can be found at:

- ∞ www.youtube.com/ playlist?list=UUpBeAfdqXHnvM4mHYcfKArw

- ∞ https://youtube.com/playlist?list=PL-xdbMjLqelLgr-1foWNRSBPoHOrowa07

- ∞ www.youtube.com/user/FinnTheInfinncible

- ∞ https://network.autism.org.uk/knowledge/ insight-opinion/gender-dysphoria-and-autism

- ∞ http://jeanette.buildsomethingpositive.com/bio.html

- ∞ www.facebook.com/watch/?v=1656725334374452

Remember, in autism, attending to several things simultaneously is difficult, so we are often socially challenged. This is why the *Diagnostic and Statistical Manual of Mental Health, fifth edition* (American Psychiatric Association, 2013) names two criteria for autism based on single attention (social and communication domain, and restrictive and repetitive interests and behaviours domain).

So, as autistic individuals, we may not discern the fuller context of OP, and interoception may be offline or connections to this eighth sense may be undetected, making self-regulation difficult. For example, we might know we packed our lunch and that it's in our lunch bag, even when we can't see it, but we might not know our family member is still around, just not within our view, if they 'disappear' to a different room in the house or go to the shop. How is it we know one concept, but not the other?

Another example of this is our ability to compartmentalize and so we can know clearly where we are and what we are doing, but if a family member has gone to the shop or is away for the weekend, it can 'feel' as if they don't exist. With our eighth sense we might have no 'awareness of feeling' about the above but it doesn't mean we don't love or miss someone. It does mean, however, that we may not connect or notice this feeling. It's common for us to lack 'big picture' thinking which requires a full range of cognitive and sensorimotor skills to work synchronously within the brain, to determine 'where am I?' and 'where is it/where are they?', especially with respect to interoception and OP.

66 {WENN} A further example of object permanence: I remember a time when I was away at university in another country, as an exchange student. My wife and family were not with me. I found it increasingly hard to know if they were still

'at home' in the country where we lived. I couldn't see them (I didn't have access to the internet at that time, or a mobile phone). I lost any sense of their existence! A friend from an autism support group encouraged me to carry a photograph and to look at it every time I wondered if they were real or not. This worked like a treat for me and helped me build a sense of 'family permanence'. You might be asking yourself what this has to do with gender and autism. Well, it has everything to do with it because it's about knowing something/someone can still exist even when we can't see them. My sense of gender has taken time to trust. I have had to find ways to help myself 'see' my true gender even when I can't 'connect' to it from looking at males in movies, pictures, magazines and so on. I am an autistic trans person who is different from many others. This is okay, but at times I need validation. 🙶

Since interoception is reduced in many of us,[2] connecting to our inner senses isn't something we are used to. If we are not good at knowing which emotion we are feeling, whether we are hungry or thirsty, sexually attracted to someone, in need of sleep, how warm or cold we are and so on, it can be very difficult to keep ourselves safe, healthy and regulated. It's also difficult to separate sensory dysphoria from gender dysphoria. Being able to do this, however, is critical to our gender journey.

In her book *A Real Person: Life on the Outside*, Swedish author Gunilla Gerland (1997) reveals how she allowed another student at school to rub her face into the snow until it bled. Gunilla explains that the boy had said to her: '...wait for me after school, I'm going to rub your face into the snow

2   https://bigabilities.com/2019/01/19/interoception-the-8th-sense-and-autism

until it bleeds'. She says she did this because the boy presented the scenario as a forgone conclusion: 'I will rub...' This kind of literal thinking is common in autism, but it can get us into all kinds of difficulty. Learning to recognize inner discomfort will help us notice and interpret our inner senses and give us some control over them. For example, if we recognize discomfort around another person, it should help us learn to avoid them or at least check in with ourselves so we can explore why we feel uncomfortable.

So, once we do understand and can connect to these very usual senses and awareness, we will be less stressed and less anxious. This ability also leads to more available attention to focus on daily learning and coping. The teaching of OP and facilitating of interoception contributes to appropriate building of the skills needed to cope with daily life. All of these skills are placed under even more pressure if we are transitioning from one gender to another.

Also, once we have the ability to connect with an understanding of our inner senses and appreciate some things still exist, even when we can't see them, it makes it easier to recognize our needs. If we can do this, it's easier to keep ourselves safe, deal with bullying and maintain a healthy sense of self.

Camouflage

On another note, the literature suggests that many autistics, especially women, are masking or camouflaging their autism. Is there compelling evidence that female autistics actually mask more than male autistics do, or is this just a post-hoc explanation we have come up with to account for under-diagnosis in females? Very little girls (e.g. toddlers) are unlikely to be masking. The very concept of masking seems to require a lot of executive functioning, which is something that isn't fully developed until early adult life, and which is poorer in autistics than neurotypicals. Yet the gender gap in diagnosis is actually the largest in early life (when autistics would be the least able to mask) and the gender ratio starts to get smaller later in life (when they would be cognitively more able to mask). So, masking seems to be a very poor explanation for the difference in gender diagnosis of autism. In particular, masking requires theory of mind. How can autistic people successfully mask if they struggle with this ability? If female autistics really do mask more than males, why is this? Is it driven by underlying social expectations of girls to be socialites and good communicators? Or conversely, is it more socially acceptable for men to be socially awkward than for women to be? Let's explore this further.

Adaptive morphing

All people will struggle to be their most intimate selves in a public setting. So, the chances are that most people develop a type of armour to take out into the social world. This is true for everyone but even more so for individuals who are already 'more different' (e.g. autistic) (Hull *et al.*, 2017). If you are not autistic and your brain is 'wired' for social skills, you may have a more 'herd-like' mentality. That is, you may recognize social norms for you and others quite easily and find you can fit into these very well. Autistic individuals, however, by the very nature of being autistic (American Psychiatric Association, 2013), may not be wired to be easily socially 'at home' among others. Picking up on social cues is more likely if you can mirror social discourse appropriately (social norm) and appreciate concepts such as 'public' and 'private' and if the social norms make sense to you. Even though in autism many of us may miss typical social signals, many also become aware of a need to find ways to keep safe. So, social 'morphing' is likely in autism if you are feeling the threat of being ostracized, bullied or at risk of other types of social power calamities.

In Western society in particular, we have an 'underlord and overlord' power imbalance (e.g. women are historically seen as inferior to men). It therefore stands to reason that where there's a power imbalance, one might learn to study the other in order to compensate. Although commonly associated with the female disposition, this is also found in any group where there is a perception of no power (e.g. child to adult).

In autism, where traditionally there has been a lack of social understanding from autistic individuals and we have gained a reputation for lacking in social skills, many have needed to become 'someone else', in order to 'fit in' (Holliday-Willey, 1999) and keep themselves from harm. In some of the literature, words such as pretending (this makes them a pretender), masking (hiding one's real self) and camouflaging (covering up or not being honest about who you truly are, which implies a conscious choice to deceive) have been used to describe this phenomenon. However, in autism such terminology is misleading because protection from perceived social threat is not born from deception but from a desire to stay safe. When it comes to gender diversity and gender transition, it's so important to know oneself. Yet, if you have spent a lifetime trying to fit in, it can be quite a riddle to unravel. If this is you, give yourself time and space to discover the 'you' that gives you a sense of being 'home'!

The many-sided self

As humans, we have many sides to our personality. Sometimes we are serious, sometimes we joke. Sometimes we are angry, sometimes we are sad, and so on. All are truly 'us', while none is complete without the other. So it's usual to be 'many sides of the same coin'. We would not state that because a person is sad one time and angry another that they are being dishonest. It's common to have different clothes to play in from those one goes to work in. Being 'appropriate' seems to come naturally for most, but for some of us there is a definite 'distance' from knowing who we really are.

When autistics are attempting to fit in or to be socially acceptable this isn't whimsical deceit, but it may be a rejection of 'self'. Very often this rejection has been taking place over many years. This can lead to an internalized dislike of self and to the attachment of shame. If shame of being autistic is your default 'self', a very real possibility of poor mental health exists. This belief, however, may not be coming from the group an individual is part of (e.g. loving family, welcoming friends) but has been established as a self-reality, over time, simply via living in a hostile society. This in turn could lead to poor mental health in a variety of guises.

66 {WENN} In general, people might think that who they are is a lot of conscience experience but who we are is also a lot of unconscious processing. Of course, who we are can take time and practice to unravel. Many of us will try on a 'persona' to see if we like it. We may practise at being 'Mummy', 'Daddy', 'a presenter' and so on. I know when I am presenting in front of an audience the comedian naturally 'comes out' and I can connect my audience to my teaching by using humour. This

isn't my usual self; this is my 'presenting self'. This aspect of me is truly me. I'm not being dishonest or using deception, I'm being the 'me' I am in that situation. "

We are all chameleons, but people under the gun have more need to morph more often!

Social armour

There are many implications for autistics when we use terms to describe our social armour. Many such terms might not be the true descriptors of the process we are going through. Such language (e.g. masking) gives the message that we are not acceptable, are deceivers and must cover our true selves.

The term camouflaging is being used to describe the actions of autistic individuals who, in trying to fit in with social situations, may be causing detachment from their true selves in the process:

> Like many autistic people, I utilize the social adaptation technique known as 'masking'. Like a chameleon that changes color in the hope of hiding from predators, an autistic person such as myself may stifle or cover up their natural body language and other ways of expressing themselves so that they might be perceived as more neurotypical. (Turk, 2020, p.60)

The end result of adaptive morphing in autism may look like another side to the self, but the language used needs to describe the process, not the product. Masking and camouflaging infer an intention and ability to deliberately and consciously pretend, deceive and cover up. But, in autism, masking can be forced on individuals as they are constantly told to 'cover' their true disposition as it is perceived as unsavoury, unnatural and unwanted. This isn't deception as initially chosen by the individual but an attempt to morph into a desired state demanded of by another to keep oneself safe (Hull *et al.*, 2017).

While on our gender discovery journey, others may say to us things like 'you never used to be like this' or 'there were no signs of this when you were younger', and this can cause us lots of doubt and discomfort and even threaten our mental health. If this describes some of your experience, do talk to a trusted friend who understands autism and gender differences, and seek the support you need.

The human need for safety is as real in autism as it is in any other human population (Platzman Weinstock, 2018). Masking (disguising) or camouflaging (using means to obscure or hide) does not fully describe the actions conferred on autistic adults who are driven by an overwhelming need to feel, and be, safe. All humans are prone to mask or pretend at times, but autistics, on a daily basis, may feel they are not allowed to be themselves when around others (Hull *et al.*, 2017). Therefore, terms such as masking and camouflaging fail to paint an appropriate picture of what is really happening for these autistic individuals whose mental health is at stake (Troxell-Whitman & Cage, 2019).

Heyworth (2018) suggests:

Ultimately, masking for me is liberating and debilitating in equal measure. I don't know how to take my masks off. I don't know how to live without masks. And they provide me with opportunities to be what I need to be for the people I love. But living a masked existence has robbed me of me. And I owe it to myself to try and find me. I owe it to the people I love to trust them enough to get to know me too. Even if I don't feel ready to 'Take My Masks Off' completely, yet.

Being socially different

When we feel, or are, socially 'different', we viscerally and intuitively know that this increases the risk of group separation or exclusion (Hull *et al.*, 2017). This exposes us to increased social, emotional and physical risk and harm. So rather than 'camouflage', we prefer 'adaptive morphing' as a state that attempts to hide us from harm, enabling us to stay and feel safe. This emerges not necessarily from an inherent or even conscious desire to deceive or pretend or mask (Lawson & Lawson, 2017) but from a desire for survival.

Some autistic people have said that they were unaware that they were modifying their behaviour to try to fit in (Lawson & Lawson, 2017). Their awareness of this only became apparent once they had heard the terms camouflaging and masking. Some have also said they were not sure how they 'naturally' responded or behaved, as they had been prevented from doing so for most of their lives (Hull *et al.*, 2017). Therefore, if adaptive morphing is not chosen but is triggered, words such as masking or camouflaging may not fully describe the processes utilized, so much as they do the outcome.

For nearly two decades, literature (e.g. Attwood, 2007; Holliday-Willey, 1999; Howlin & Moss, 2012; Hull *et al.*, 2017; Lai *et al.*, 2017; Livingston, Shah & Happé, 2019) and personal blogs (e.g. Nirode, 2018) have been referring to some individuals on the autism spectrum as being able to camouflage, pretend, mask and blend in, in order to fit into social or other settings and to appear normal (Holliday-Willey, 1999). Now, more and more literature (e.g. Cage, Di Monaco & Newell, 2018; Cassidy *et al.*, 2018; Lai *et al.*, 2017; Troxell-Whitman & Cage, 2019) is demonstrating the negative impact such behaviour has on the mental health and well-being of those autistic adults by showing that their mental health was negatively impacted by camouflaging their autism.

Language

Words are powerful. They shape – and are shaped by – our assumptions, perspectives and concepts (e.g. Ronch & Thomas, 2009). As such, words can unintentionally lead others to certain beliefs or positions which may not be true, accurate or helpful. For example, snow, snowflake and avalanche all relate to 'snow' but they infer very different ideas about the shared concept of the frozen white stuff. When positioning oneself with certain terminology or expressions, we need to consider the outcome. In using the powerful tool of language, it is our responsibility to make sure that the words truly represent an individual's or group's reality, are appropriate, and are not simply the language of the majority.

Language includes a person's pronouns and the name they choose to be called. Transphobia is often demonstrated and perpetrated through the intentional misgendering and dead-naming of a person. Conversely, using the correct name and pronouns is an indicator of respect.

Words, social attitudes and belief

Social attitudes have always influenced language and vice versa (e.g. Preston, 2011). Appreciating that language impacts discourse and influences attitudes is important because it will impact how we view ourselves and our gender journey. Language influences power, and power determines who gets to have a say, what types of power are used and what access to rights, obligations and duties an individual or a group may exhibit. Stigma may be behind the social pressure that pushes us to feel the need to mask. Stigmatization is conceptualized as a socio-cultural process which operates to reproduce structural power relationships and exclude stigmatized individuals from the social world (Parker & Aggleton, 2003). So we need to take our power and use it wisely!

Today, person-first language (e.g. person with autism) is increasingly being exchanged for identity-first language (e.g. autistic person). This has been driven by the autistic majority, concerned that phrases like person with autism suggest that autism can somehow be separated from them, allowing the person (without autism) to be seen. Therefore, person-first language is viewed by many autistics as misleading and an inaccurate description of who they really are. The authors of this book are concerned that words used to describe some autistics' coping strategies are misleading too. It could be argued this is in much the same way as person-first language might be misleading.

With this awareness, we note that some autistics may notice social intention and predict a socially acceptable response. However, most of us will have difficulties with this due to poor object permanence (Lawson & Dombroski, 2017), poor interoceptive connection (Goodall, 2019) and be very much one-tracked or single-focused in our attention and experience (Lawson, 2011).

Less small talk

Therefore, autistic ways of interacting socially are often observed to involve less small talk and social niceties, and more specific and focused interactions concerning topics of mutual interest. This behaviour is at odds with normative social expectations and can often lead to the strengths of this ability to focus and specialize being ignored or dismissed as too intense or too personal and not socially acceptable. Yet it is often these very traits that set us apart which can be our greatest strengths and enable us to be compassionate, empathetic, direct, focused and productive; see, for example, Greta Thunberg's view on her diagnosis of Asperger syndrome.[3]

Survival

As mentioned previously, people's responses to a perceived threat can be fight, flight, freeze, flop, fawn and possibly morph. Social exclusion can be a strong and visceral perceived or actual threat. The authors believe that our human in-built survival mechanisms are prompts that trigger many autistics to seek and enact socially acceptable observed, rather than intuitive, thoughts and behaviours to stay safe. In this way, this marginalized group is finding a social solution to the social problem of being subjected to unspoken social rules and expectations which we experience as a culture of negative

---

3   www.theguardian.com/environment/2019/sep/02/greta-thunberg-responds-to-aspergers-critics-its-a-superpower

experiences and expectations, from the dinner table, to the classroom, to the shop floor (Wood, 2019).

In a world where non-autistics are the majority, their social interaction style is considered the acceptable one. This norm is based on the functions of a brain wired to enable social connection in a manner used by most of the non-autistic population as they divide attention and share across multiple (polytropic) interests (Murray, Lesser & Lawson, 2005). This is only possible because of its communication system, which allows for attention to multiple foci at once, which leads to a set of behaviours that are valued and rewarded by the neuro-majority. Some of these are appropriate eye contact, appropriate facial expression, appropriate reading of body language, and connected interoceptive awareness (Lawson, 2011; Lawson & Dombroski, 2017). Autistic social behaviours and preferences which differ from societal norms are pathologized and called a disorder or condition, as they do not conform to these normative ascribed styles. This has a heap of implications for the intersectionality of autism and gender diversity. For example, some individuals say things like 'I don't feel like a man or a woman, I feel like me', others may say, 'I know my physical body looks like male (or female), but actually I'm both', and so on.

People who are naturally able to conform to society's social expectations have no need to behave in a way contrary to their nature in order to be socially acceptable and rewarded. Many autistics choose to act in ways contrary to their natural behaviours in order to increase their chances of social inclusion and, thus, decrease their risk of negative consequences from the non-autistic majority.

Is this, however, a deliberate deception or a survival

strategy cultivated over many years? Is this a conscious act or a subconscious response to real or perceived trauma? Yes, many autistics cover up aspects of themselves they wish to keep hidden, as a response to trauma. Sometimes this involves our gender identity.

66 {WENN} For me, sometimes this is done subconsciously; rarely is it done deliberately. In fact, it's only as we talk together that I realize I have been doing this over many years.

I don't think my intention is to deceive others into thinking I'm something I'm not, it's more about trying to do what I've been told. Or, not do what my family have told me to contain. 99

Many autistics will focus on the things that matter to them rather than being and doing social, unless social is an aspect of their interest. Also, it is important to note that the human brain – whether Autistic or Neurotypical – manages best when it can focus on one thing at any one time (Gopher, Armony & Greenspan, 2000).

As well as being seen as a socially mediated skill, autistic coping and adaptation could also be seen as biologically programmed and activated in order to keep oneself safe. Often, we observe others to see what it is that they do. As we practise these ways, we note what works and what does not work. For example, for anticipatory or current social discomfort, some autistics may use demand-avoidant methods such as refusal to cooperate, pleading inability, or controlling a situation to enable escape and increase comfort. Alternatively, they may choose to interact in a defensive, competitive or combative way. Some may prefer to morph and adapt their behaviour to mimic non-autistic strategies that they have seen in attempts to create social connection, success and reward from others. This morphing can be compared to tactics used by the majority of chameleons.

Adaptive morphing in nature

Nature teaches us many things about ways to survive, and one lizard particularly begs our attention. It is the chameleon. Chameleon is a term used to describe a certain type of highly specialized lizard. It is an old-world clade, meaning it is from a single source heritage, but with multiple presentations. Chameleons have been around a very long time. So has autism[4] (Feinstein, 2010). There are many interesting things about chameleons, one being that many can change their colour to match their surroundings and circumstances. However, this is not a chosen activity so much as a means built into their biology, which is usually triggered by environmental temperature and perceived threat (Edmonds, 2015).

When we compare the chameleon's threat response to autistic morphing, we are closer to understanding the strategies some autistics use to help them navigate social situations and expectations. Because of the intrinsically human desire to belong, many autistics are drawn by both biology and necessity to be included with, and accepted by, the non-autistic majority (Baldwin, Costley & Warren, 2013). This may contribute to years of living in the wrong gender, with a desire not to upset others always taking priority over exploration of what we need to do for ourselves. However, without true inclusive adjustments that allow for genuine inclusion and acceptance,

---

4   www.parents.com/health/autism/the-history-of-autism

this desire will continue to be thwarted by the stigma that is still associated with autism. As long as our society lacks truly inclusive attitudes and practices, autistics will need to continue to display chameleon-like responses in socially threatening situations. Our mental, emotional, physical and financial lives depend on it.

Cis-female autistics?

In recent publications, including one of Wenn's (Lawson, 2017), the words masking and camouflaging are used to explain why females on the spectrum have remained invisible and do not figure in either historical or recent statistics. Initially, it was reasoned that they failed to show in the data because autism is predominantly a male condition (Asperger, cited in Frith, 1992). In later years, it was argued females were more immune to autism because of the properties of oestrogen which gave them a certain protection against becoming autistic (Constantino & Charman, 2012). More recently, females are said to use masking and camouflage to hide their difficulties (Lai *et al.*, 2017).

Biologically, due to inherent attributes on the XX chromosome, autistic females, and females in general, tend to be more social (Head, McGillivray & Stokes, 2014). Females are able to notice and use more acceptable social behaviours, because certain behaviours appear to be more available to them than they are to those without the XX chromosome (Cox *et al.*, 2015). This suggests that, from a young age, autistic girls may have noticed others and learned how to act as if they understood normative and expected social motivation, dynamics and behaviours, even when they did not. Therefore, their actions act as a mask that covers their real difficulties. However, in this scenario, masking and camouflage may not be a chosen state or a conscious act. Rather, it is the result of enacted behaviour to avoid the discomfort of not fitting in, or fear of being punished or shunned, and may have happened almost automatically, without conscious awareness, planning or control.

As well as avoiding discomfort in social situations by adapting behaviour, autistic females can appear to have a level of social ability that adheres to normative expectations. This may then reduce the level of discomfort that others have with them. Additionally, often autistic females have specific passionate interests that are more commonly accepted as typical in any female. These could be a passion for books, animals, people, art, fashion, theatre or music. As these pursuits are often appreciated and rewarded by society for females, they may not be recognized as being particularly single-focused or rigid. As a result, their autistic characteristics may pass unnoticed (Carpenter, Happé & Egerton, 2019; Lawson, 1998). We find it interesting that some trans women may have been more drawn to traditional feminine things during their growing-up years, which is also seen in autism, than they were to traditional boy things.

Due to the above scenario, autistic females may also have more internalizing psychological characteristics than autistic males, such as anxiety or depression. They may also have more self-directed symptoms like self-blame and low self-worth, and fewer externalizing behaviours such as aggression or challenging behaviours that are more typical of autistic males. Such variable and critical difficulties may commonly go unnoticed by parents or teachers.

Unfortunately, in the long term, these behaviours and strategies which lead to females remaining unidentified as autistic can often lead to their mental health being negatively impacted. As a result, females are more often misdiagnosed with other issues such, as depression, personality disorders, social phobia, eating disorders and anxiety disorders, than are autistic males (e.g. Eaton, 2017; Lawson, 2017; National Autistic Society (NAS) 2019). They are also much more likely to have these as comorbidities (Lawson, 2017). This could mean the psychological issues may be supported, but the underlying autistic cause may not be addressed, compromising the ability to create sustainable and positive mental health and identity outcomes. With history showing that females fare less well in many situations compared to males, there is even more concern that words should truly represent autistic experience.

When we take this understanding and apply it to those who are living with gender dysphoria and who are transitioning, as they look back over their lives it is interesting that many have a much-aligned brain disposition to that seen in cis-females and males:

In their study, Dr Julie Bakker from the University of Liège, Belgium, and her colleagues from the Center of Expertise on Gender Dysphoria at the VU University Medical Center, the Netherlands, examined sex differences in the brain activation patterns of young transgender people. The study included both adolescent boys and girls with gender dysphoria and used magnetic resonance imaging scans to assess brain activation patterns in response to a pheromone known to produce gender-specific activity. The pattern of brain activation in both transgender adolescent boys and girls more closely resembled that of non-transgender boys and girls of their desired gender. In addition, GD adolescent girls showed a male-typical brain activation pattern during a visual/spatial memory exercise. Finally, some brain structural changes were detected that were also more similar, but not identical, to those typical of the desired gender of GD boys and girls. (European Society of Endocrinology, 2018)

Camouflage may well have been a cover that many of us have survived behind, not born from an intention to deceive but rather a learned or intuitive outcome to maintain safety.

One day, autism will be recognized for the norm that it is, for many individuals. It will, therefore, be the norm to see individuals wearing sunglasses or tinted lenses or a baseball cap when inside; the norm to use a weighted garment or soft toy to aid relaxation; the norm for individuals to choose not to be social unless sharing a mutual interest; and the norm to be themselves without the need to hide who they truly are. One day, gender won't be a dividing factor so much as an individual one, which is expected as the norm for that person.

CHAPTER 6

Older Autistic
Trans Adults

Introduction

This chapter briefly explores a number of experiences related
to older autistic adults who discover their gender identity later
in life. These might be trans autistic adults or autistic adults
who finally connect to an understanding that their gender
identity is different from the one they have grown up with, as
identified by others and adhered to by themselves. In autism,
it's common for many to do or be what others say they should
do or be (Gerland, 2003; Lawson, 2000; Purkis, 2006). This is
doubly dangerous when it comes to vulnerability in issues of
abuse or being led into activity of a dubious nature due to not
comprehending the consequences. An adult of typical intellect
and not autistic may recognize this vulnerability and exploit
it. In the non-autistic population, recognizing gender variance
and dysphoria may occur earlier, simply because seeing the big
picture in autism (connecting to one's thoughts, emotions and
wider societal expectations plus personal autonomy) can take

longer due to accessing these via a different operating system (Fletcher-Watson & Happé, 2019; Lawson, 2011).

What issues do trans and gender-diverse autistic adults face?

Some issues that trans and gender-diverse autistic people often experience include:

∞ *Prejudice and bigotry.* This can occur in any setting such as within families, at work, and even in the autistic community. Bigotry can range from deliberate misgendering to the use of violence. As autistic people are often subjected to bigotry and discrimination anyway, additional bigotry levelled at them for being trans and gender diverse can be particularly traumatic. It should be noted that bigotry is never okay and is never the fault of the victim.

∞ *Intersectionality.* Many autistic and trans and gender-diverse people also belong to other intersectional groups. They may be a person of colour, be economically disadvantaged, or have a mental illness and a range of other 'differences'. Intersectionality compounds disadvantage and discrimination. A person may identify more strongly with other intersectional identities than being autistic or trans. These other areas may be their main concern or interest in terms of their identity. Being aware of intersectionality – and privilege – is an important part of understanding yourself, or another person, and treating them with respect. It also relates to the need for understanding societal issues around discrimination and power.

∞ *Self-doubt.* Trans and gender-diverse people often doubt that their identity is 'right' and question their own judgement and reality. This is often compounded by inappropriate messages from others, especially for people who come to affirm their gender at older ages. This self-doubt can cause a person to question their gender and worry that their trans experience is 'just a phase'. Given the infantilization and control from others that autistic people so often face, this can be even more prominent for those who are trans and gender diverse, especially those who have higher support needs.

∞ *Difficulties accessing supports and services.* This is an issue for autistic people generally. Necessary supports may not be respectful or inclusive for autistic people. Services – such as health care – may be inaccessible due to cost or sensory accessibility issues. For some trans and gender-diverse autistic people, clinicians supporting transition can be ableist and dismiss autistic people. This is a significant issue for those who experience it as it can be seen as a betrayal and leave autistic people feeling isolated and unsupported. In addition, there is the possibility of not being allowed to access medical treatment to support their transition.

∞ *People's experience of being autistic and trans can be invalidated and dismissed, including by health professionals.* While self-doubt is a significant issue, a similar problem is where autistic people are invalidated or dismissed when they talk about their gender. Self-doubt is bad enough, but when combined with others invalidating and dismissing them then their self-doubt is essentially confirmed, sometimes by an apparent 'expert'. If you gather all your strength in order to come out as trans and then someone you respect dismisses it, that is a considerable problem and also a betrayal.

∞ *Mental illness/suicidal ideation.* Many autistic people and many trans and gender-diverse people experience poor mental health and suicidal ideation. Being trans and gender diverse itself is *not* a mental illness and neither is autism, but many trans and gender-diverse people experience mental illness in addition to their other experiences. These are significant problems often requiring support and treatment. There are a number of mental health supports for LGBTQIA+ people, including QLife in Australia.[1] If you are experiencing suicidal thoughts or mental health issues it is important to access support.

∞ *Being misgendered.* Misgendering is a big issue for trans and gender-diverse people. Some people may be bigoted and deliberately misgender people and others may do so unintentionally. When intentional,

---

1   www.facebook.com/qlifeaus

it is a form of invalidation, where a person's sense of self and identity is overlooked or intentionally challenged. For many of us, it is hard to call out misgendering for a variety of reasons – we don't want to upset the other person or cause them to be angry with us, we may not have the confidence to say something or we may be doubting who we are and so struggle to raise the issue. Misgendering can happen every day and is frustrating and upsetting.

Answers to some common questions about autism and gender diversity

Trans and gender-diverse autistic people frequently come up against others' unhelpful assumptions and misconceptions. These can be hurtful or triggering or just plain irritating. Some misconceptions and some possible responses are listed here.

Why did you wait until you were 60 to work out you were trans?

We live in a world which is not very inclusive of trans people and their experiences. While this attitude is changing for children and young people, for older adults, being trans may never have been presented as an option. They may have had no frame of reference for their gender identity as there was no information about being trans available to them until recently. Those identities simply did not exist in the way we know them now. The only gender identity presented was cis-male or cis-female, so people tried to fit into that as much as possible despite it taking a huge toll on their sense of self and identity.

Many older people have discovered their gender identity at quite late an age simply because they have become aware that there are options available to them which they hadn't considered in the past. It might also be the case that, as an older adult, they are in a position to 'act' on their newly appreciated connection, meaning they can emotionally, physically and financially attend to this awareness and make informed choices as to what they can do about it. As younger people, many autistic adults were simply not in a place to act on any developing understanding because of other situations, such as still being dependent on family, being in a relationship and family that depended on them or being employed in a place which might have meant the loss of their job if they had revealed their growing concerns.

Those who transition later in life may have been thinking about their gender for a long time. They may have struggled to come out due to bigotry, discrimination and self-doubt. Attitudes are changing, but historically coming out as trans was not considered okay by workplaces and individuals in the general population. As autistic people tend to experience a lot of prejudice and discrimination anyway, many autistic adults may have felt unable to come out as trans as it would only compound the discrimination they already faced. Recent developments in gender diversity that have allowed for it being more socially accepted could have resulted in older trans and gender-diverse autistic people feeling okay to come out for the first time.

As well as the above, joining the dots for autistic individuals may take longer than for non-autistic individuals (Lawson & Lawson, 2017). Autism involves developmental delays and sensory profiles not conducive to seeing the overall picture. For example, Wenn needed to separate the different sensory discomforts he lived with into those which were problematic because he is autistic and those which were due to living with gender dysphoria.

66 {WENN} For most of my life I had 'lumped' the considerations of having sensory issues around my body and having gender dysphoria together beneath the umbrella of autism. I only came to understand that having my then 'breasts' out of bounds to my partner was more to do with not accepting them as part of me than it was part of sensory discomfort. The first time a trans autistic friend shared this with me, as part of his experience, the light went on. I am now sure of this as my partner has complete access to my now male chest and I don't grit my teeth if she is close to it! 99

You have only just come out at the age of 50. Isn't that confusing for everyone that knows you?

The idea that gender identity will confuse people – children or adults – is a harmful one. It is often a form of bigotry by stealth. If someone is confused by a person's gender they should learn more about gender diversity rather than blame a trans person for their 'confusion'. Would you blame a person of colour for racism? One would hope not! Pronouns and names can be learned over time even by someone who has genuine trouble remembering to use the correct ones. The 'confusion' argument often comes from a place of bigotry. If you think about this idea of confusion in context it doesn't really stack up. For example, if someone got married and took their spouse's name, would that be 'confusing'? Older people transitioning can come up against a lot of discussion around 'but I've always known you as...so that is who you are to me'.

The respectful and right thing to do is to use their correct pronouns and name and view them as their affirmed gender.

Why do you need to be non-binary? You
have been a woman for 45 years!

Gender identity is a core part of who someone is. People can affirm gender at any age. It is just as necessary for a 45-year-old gender-diverse person to affirm their gender as it is for a young person. Simple length of time of living as a cis-person is not an argument as to why someone should not affirm their gender. In fact, for many older people who are trans and gender diverse, there is a great urgency to transition. Realizing their true identity after decades can be a liberating thing but also a very difficult time. To know that decades have gone by when you could have been yourself but weren't able to be can be very difficult to assimilate. In relation to the question around someone having expressed their gender in one way for many years and then transitioning, it is important to note that trans and non-binary gender identities are valid for people at any age.

You're autistic. Doesn't that mean you are confused about
your identity anyway? There's lots of autistic trans people
now, so maybe you are just jumping on the bandwagon?

Usually a person who affirms their gender diversity knows who they are. The sheer pressure from society to conform to the cisgender binary usually means that if someone has come to the realization they are trans then they are almost certainly correct. Trans and autistic people are likely to be aware of who they are, given that they tend to spend a lot of time reflecting on the nature of their identity! It is a huge invalidation to tell someone that their trans identity is 'wrong' and is a very disrespectful thing to say. It is also insulting and wrong to assume that autistic people have disordered identities and will simply come out as trans because someone else did.

You said that you started to transition years ago but then stopped. If that's the case, how do you know you really want to now?

First, a person's decision to transition is their own and not up for discussion or dispute from other people. There are many different reasons a person would delay or postpone their transition including their often very real concern about bigotry or discrimination. For example, some people's decision has been the difference between transitioning or keeping their job. This is not an easy or flippant choice and being questioned for it does not help anyone. Transitioning can be filled with challenges and is generally not one simple decision. Rather than questioning their motives, it is better to support a person who has had to delay their transition. Judging them is most likely done from ignorance, and getting to know an individual may help to answer this question.

Affirming gender – practical strategies

Coming out to family members

As stated in an earlier chapter, the coming out conversation with family members is likely to be a difficult one, depending on the attitudes of those you are coming out to. Coming out to family – parents, siblings, children – can be very challenging and anxiety-provoking. Here are some tips that might help:

∞ *Be honest and clear.* This is you talking about something very important to you. Include things like how you feel about gender and how you have felt about gender in the past, and why you are affirming your gender – how it makes you feel to be yourself and why it is a good thing. You can also talk about how you want to be referred to and what your expectations from family members are.

∞ *Don't be ashamed.* Being trans and gender diverse is a natural part of being human. It is not something to fear or be ashamed of. You are not doing the wrong thing, 'sinning' or being deliberately difficult. Your transition is not about other people, it is about you. Remind yourself that you have the right to be who you are, your true self.

∞ *Don't apologize for being yourself.* As your gender is not a reason for shame, it is also not a reason for apology. If someone finds using your pronouns or name difficult then that is about them and they need to change it. If anything, they should apologize to you for not supporting and acknowledging your gender. Once again, remind yourself that you have the right to be who you are.

∞ *Plan what you are going to say.* In a practical sense, coming out is a conversation. Like any potentially difficult conversation, preparation is key. You can have a think about what you want to say and anticipate any questions you think you will be asked. You can even put some guiding points on paper and bring that to the conversation. You can practise these with a supportive friend or by speaking out loud while looking in the mirror.

∞ *Plan the setting in which you will have the coming out conversation.* Given that this is 'your' conversation and it is potentially going to be difficult, plan where and when you are going to have it. Do it where it feels right for you, somewhere you feel comfortable and in control. You may want to invite family members to your home. While it can be a conversation people have in the spur of the moment, it is often better to plan it in order to have more control over the conversation. Try to ensure that the environment for the conversation is calming and not overwhelming in terms of sensory input or negative past associations. It might even be of benefit to have a support person with you.

∞ *Be prepared for questions.* It is almost guaranteed that you will receive some questions from family members. Some of these will probably be out of genuine interest and others may betray hostility, depending on the attitudes of your family members. You can tell family members that you may need to come back and answer their questions at a later date if you are feeling overwhelmed. Try to not assume that all the questions are hostile. However, if a question is hostile or you experience it as such, try to set a boundary and tell the person who asked it that their question is not appropriate and you will not answer it. You need to look after yourself. You have no obligation to respond to disrespectful questions.

∞ *Be aware that people can change their views over time.* Even if a family member is not supportive, this may change in time.

∞ *Be assertive.* Assertiveness can make the coming-out process more manageable. Being able to set boundaries around how people respond to you is your prerogative. For example, you are in control! Assertiveness is a quality which many people improve at as they grow older. There are training courses around learning assertiveness and it is something a counsellor can usually assist with. In fact, having a good therapist is an essential part of this journey.

Managing relationships with family/children

Relationships with family and children can be tricky for many autistic people, but being trans and gender diverse can add to this difficulty. Here are some tips for promoting positive relationships:

∞ *Set and respect boundaries where you can.* You have the right to be accepted and respected. If family members say inappropriate and hurtful things then you have the right to call them out on it or avoid spending time with them.

∞   *Protect yourself.* For some people that means setting
and maintaining boundaries, while for others it means
distancing yourself from biological family and finding
or initiating a family of choice whose members love
and respect you.

∞   *Remember that your children (if you have them) may well
love and respect you in any situation.* Where children are
disrespectful to a trans parent it is often the result
of other family members modelling disrespectful
thinking and behaviour. Children can find the
negative attitudes and behaviours family members
may have around someone transitioning upsetting
and confusing. It should be noted that transitioning
is unlikely to cause confusion among children in
and of itself and those attitudes where transitioning
confuses children are often born out of prejudice and
transphobia rather than concerns around their parent
transitioning (Veldorale-Griffin, 2014).

∞   *Expect respect.* It can be very difficult for autistic people
to know if family members are being respectful or not.
Neurotypical people tend to do better at working out
people's motivation than autistics might. Sometimes
it can help to do a reality check and ask for
clarification from a family member if you are not sure
whether they are being rude. It can also help to check
with a trusted friend about situations and whether
someone's behaviour was respectful or not.

∞   *Try not to catastrophize* about relationship issues if your family is respectful and accepting. Every family has tension and difficulties; people argue and disagree. The chances are the issues will resolve in time in a respectful family.

∞   *Understand why you might be misgendered.* You may find that your family members misgender you. This can be very complicated and family members sometimes do things that you would not tolerate from friends or colleagues. Each person is different and manages this issue differently, but a general rule is to try and find the intent behind the misgendering. If your family members plainly love you but call you 'son' because they remember you as such despite you being female, it is probably quite different from them refusing to accept your gender and pronouns because they are bigots. This is one of those tricky areas of nuance and subtlety and should be considered in each instance. It can be possible to educate family members about using correct names and pronouns, especially if you articulate how upsetting and hurtful it can be when they misgender you.

∞   *Challenge assumptions of others about autism.* Being autistic can result in assumptions of incompetence and paternalism. If you are an autistic person in a disempowered position, being trans can exacerbate those existing issues. Many people find themselves needing to educate their families about autism and gender diversity. If this is you it can be important to be in contact with your autistic or neurodivergent peers to ensure that you have someone to vent to and work through any issues with.

CASE EXAMPLE: COMING OUT TO OLDER PARENTS

Del is 45, autistic and recently came out as gender fluid. They had known for many years that their gender did not conform to the binary notion of gender but didn't articulate that at a conscious level. They started a conversation around gender with an autistic trans friend and after some consideration realized they were non-binary. Del was okay with coming out to other friends but was very concerned about having the conversation with their parents who are elderly and conservative Christians. However, Del wanted to come out to their parents as this was being true to themselves, but they were very concerned about the impact it might have on their parents and the negative response Del may have to deal with.

Del practised the coming out conversation with their friend a few times which helped them feel more comfortable about it. They then arranged to meet their parents face to face and explained how they felt. They explained they had always been aware they don't conform to traditional notions of gender. Del's parents responded better than expected but it was a very hard conversation to have. Del's mum was focused on pronouns and how she would 'get them wrong' and 'it will be really hard for me'. Del's dad didn't say much but in the proceeding months said he sort of understood. Del was relieved that their parents weren't hostile but also felt that their parents made everything about 'them' rather than understanding how Del felt. Three months later Del's mum still hadn't used their correct pronouns which Del found hurtful. However, Del is viewing the conversation with their parents as an ongoing one and hoping to get to a place where there is greater understanding.

Being yourself

Everyone is different and each person's experience will vary. The important thing is to be able to live with 'yourself'.

66 {WENN} For the longest time, I put others first and lived my life according to the rules of those I mixed with. I remember watching a film and one of the adults said to another, 'From where I sit you are way out of your league.' To which the former adult replied, 'I think you should change your seat.' At that moment, it occurred to me that simply being with a certain group who have particular views doesn't mean those views are the only ones. It might simply mean the other views haven't been considered yet. 99

Giving yourself licence to further explore and check out why you have particular feelings is all part of the journey. Dating someone doesn't automatically mean you will marry them, it just means you are trying someone on for size. If it's not a good fit, you draw your conclusions and move on.

Strategies or ways of thinking and acting that might add to the clues for understanding who we are

How can we know if we are trans? Take a test to check out what your sensory profile is. It might be best to visit a professional who can do this with you. Once you know how you experience your sensory information you can separate your experience into different veins. For example, outward expression is affected by *touch*, for example closeness of people. But, what happens if I touch my own arm, my chest, my hair and so on? Is there a difference? If I feel uncomfortable with my own body, but I can touch most of me, are there places I don't like to touch (breasts, genitals)? If so, this might be more connected to gender dysphoria than to sensory dysphoria.

Inward expression is affected by *sight*, for example looking in the mirror. Emotionally, I might feel sad, angry, uncomfortable and so on if I look in a mirror. This might be thought of as a visual sense of discomfort. But not liking to look at your own image could be connected to your gender identity. For example, does this change if you dress differently? How do you feel if you dress in traditionally female or male clothing? Can you look in a mirror when wearing some clothes but not if you are wearing others?

Separating sensory experiences is important as indicators of gender dysphoria, because as autistics we may have not recognized that these exist for us. We have so many sensory discomforts it's easy to miss them.

The various thoughts, ideas, experiences and insights in the above conversation are just some to consider. Remember that we are all different and not everyone will fit into the same frame. Finding where you fit and what works for you may take a bit of trial and error; after all, it's not as if we are all practised at this. Being an older autistic individual who has come late (but in the right time for you) to an understanding of your gender, you will need to be patient with yourself and with others.

Emergency situations

Ageing in a social world that does not accommodate autistic adults' thinking, processing and learning styles means that at least one autistic person in one hundred is being dehumanized. The talk about inclusion is causing exclusion for a growing population and this amounts to a developing disaster for those affected. It could be different. With the gaining of an understanding specific to our population, and appropriately based practice, this can change. Autistic individuals are often prone to the impact of sensory overload (or underload) on perception and the ability to respond to information. For example, the needs of people on the spectrum are often missed in the delivery of messages geared towards the non-autistic population. This isn't just so in the case of gender discovery, but in all aspects of information delivery. But if you don't know this is you, it can be difficult to explain to others.

We don't need to apologize for our brain dispositions or sensory processing styles though, we just need to accept that this is us and it's how we are. So, if you need help decoding the specific information you need when it comes to medical jargon or social expectations, knowing who to ask or where to go is your right. If your local GP can't help you or even your local gender community centre doesn't seem to have the knowledge on being autistic and living with gender differences, your gender therapist or specialist should know who to contact. Also, your local Autistic & Trans Facebook group can probably help too.

There are a number of 'emergency' situations where we might find it difficult to express our needs and this is important because we need to plan ahead.

66 {WENN} When I was going for my transgender surgery the surgeon asked me a number of questions that I needed to have a plan for. Some of them were things like: 'Do you have

enough credit on your credit card, if your surgery uncovers complications and the procedure ends up costing more?' Other issues I hadn't considered concerned what to do and who to contact should there be a need to, such as who I considered to be my next of kin? Other examples were, did I have a living will, or any other type of will? These issues really need us to have the appropriate conversations with family and put necessary insurances in place, so we can plan ahead. 99

66 {YENN} I have a mental illness and have had to access inpatient mental health services on a number of occasions. Explaining my pronouns and gender identity is usually very difficult in these situations and I find myself being misgendered most of the time. On the rare occasions that staff attempt my pronouns they tend to follow correct usage by saying how challenging it is for them to do so! 99

What to do if, what to do when, and how to do it

Then there are those of us with intellectual challenges who may need visual information so we can access understanding better than spoken or written information. These stories need to be part of someone's routine and practised often. They can also be placed into role-play and 'acted out'. When an individual is 'at home' with a procedure and not taken by surprise they will be more likely to participate. Surprises in autism tend to be scary and unwanted, and potentially increase stress rather than be experienced as fun. Individuals may be more at risk of panic and of doing the thing they have been told not to do, when surprised.

If individuals experience sensory overload they may become catatonic and not be able to move. It's as if the over-whelmed system closes down and words sound like someone speaking under water! Vision may be a blur and touch may feel like being stung! No amount of reasoning with an individual will enable them to respond appropriately. All sharing of the information we need to know needs to be conveyed to us in ways that suit our learning styles. This might be verbal for some, others will prefer pictures and photographs, while others need story for using words, pictures, symbols. If we are not sure of our learning style, we can explore all and see which connects us best. So what to do if, what to do when and how to do it will depend on who we are, what ways we learn best (so material can be presented to us in ways that make sense) and when the right time exists for all if this to happen. It might be more uncomfortable presenting too much information to us in one go, or some will want the whole story given to them so they can choose how they navigate it.

CHAPTER 7

Strategies and Tips
to Promote Pride
and Strength

Knowing the difference between assertiveness, rudeness, being anti-social and lording it over another isn't always an easy affair! We need to be assertive and clear about what we need, and we need to know how to address bigotry and promote self-respect and self-worth. We also need to be able to separate the differences. Feeling good about who we are and how we need to live our life, respectfully and with pride, is our right and finding appropriate ways to do this isn't always easy. This chapter looks at this and gives you some ideas on how to do this, and how to do it well. It also addresses some of the issues around social and surgical transition.

Advocacy, rights and education

As already expressed in previous chapters, in autism, not only are we wired differently from the non-autistic population but various research on our brains is saying interesting things that help us feel good about who we are. In autism, we exhibit particular brain patterns that show up in certain brain imaging technology. These patterns suggest that exploring autistic strengths rather than weaknesses is beneficial to us all (Blair, 2006; Dawson *et al.*, 2007). This way of thinking about autism positively maximizes the choice, voice and control of autistic individuals. For example, enabling access to the supports we need might mean utilizing types of software from technology.

66 {WENN} When it's been difficult to use my voice, I can, for example, use *Proloquo2Go*. This software from iTunes allows me to choose pictures which are converted to text and then spoken by the software (pictures to speech). In this way, I can have a say about what my needs are, what I am feeling and what I hope can happen for me. 99

However, advances in brain technology might allow science to explore brain functioning and highlight areas of difference between the generic brain and the autistic brain, but this doesn't necessarily translate to improved acceptance and accommodation for us. Many of us, as autistic individuals, have proved our value to society because of the commitment to single-focused interest/occupation. This obsessive nature, rightly channelled, has shown undoubted value in areas of science, education, music, the arts, engineering, mathematics, computer technology and so on. But, being 'able' doesn't equal value! We are valuable because we are! You are valuable just because you exist. You have the right to explore and to know your gender identity, even if it's different from the one you were assigned at birth.

Ultimately, brain imaging technology has significantly enhanced the lives of autistic individuals, because it demonstrates our abilities. We are not just a bunch of deficits. We have the technology that can enable communication between us, even if speech is absent. However, some still believe that autism is a bundle of challenging behaviours and this colours their vision and takes away the individual's control over their own lives. Moving on from this outdated thinking style is helpful because it should mean doctors and professionals take us seriously rather than doubt that we are the ones who know our needs best. But we may need support in knowing how to do this.

Advocacy is all about speaking with confidence to address those things you might need. It could mean adaptations at college or at work, and it is your right to ask for these. It might mean having an advocate speak on your behalf if you don't feel confident, or it might mean using technology to enable you to type the words you would like to say. Whatever way you choose that might work for you, this is okay.

Autistic pride and trans pride

Pride is an important element of well-being and self-esteem for trans and gender-diverse autistic people. Pride is premised on the idea that difference should be respected and celebrated. *It echoes the notion that people have the right to be who they are.* Pride is often seen as a community sentiment or a political act, but it is also an important element of an individual's life. Cultivating a sense of pride can help to counter transphobia and bigotry and result in people being able to like and value themselves as they are. Pride is a useful counter to hatred because it is harder to bully a person who has a strong sense of pride and who genuinely likes and values themselves.

Pride has historical roots and they are frequently related to political struggles for respect and acceptance. Being proud as an autistic person and as a trans person is a positive disposition. Pride sets an example for others to be empowered by. Pride is a right.

Gender diversity and the autistic community

While many autistic people are very respectful of difference and respond positively to gender diversity, there are bigots in any community, including ours. Some people are hostile to trans and gender-diverse people for reasons of conscious transphobia and hate, and some can be bigoted for other reasons. These include believing gender diversity is somehow 'new' and they 'cannot keep up'. For others, it's about coming from demographic groups which do not have language for or understanding of gender diversity. However, this is not an excuse, and people in the current day have a responsibility to be respectful of transgender people as they do of all other people.

It can feel worse to experience bigotry and transphobia from others in the autistic community given that they face discrimination too and should presumably know better. Being autistic is not an excuse for being bigoted. The autistic community should be supportive of trans and gender-diverse people.

What to do when people in the autistic/autism community are bigoted:

∞ If you can, call them out on it.

∞ Share material promoting respect and pride.

∞ Get together with other autistic trans and gender-diverse people – you are not alone.

∞ Explain why it is not okay and how it makes you feel.

∞ Support people and groups promoting respect and pride.

On the positive side, the autistic community can be very supportive and inclusive and can be a place of safety for trans and gender-diverse autistic people. However, it is wise to be aware that this is not always the response.

❝ {YENN} When I came out as non-binary in 2018 I shared the news on social media. Many people were very supportive, but a few people were bigoted, including autistic people. A friend told me coming out would show me who were friends and who were not, but I hadn't realized how true that statement was until I came out. I was very disappointed and sad that autistic people were among the bigots as I had hoped they would understand difference and diversity. ❞

Yenn's journey – early experiences of non-binary pride

❝ {YENN} The other day at work I saw an email from my workplace's Pride network, which I am note-taker for. The survey was about coming out at work for those who identify as one or more of the letters in the LGBTQIA+ acronym. I have identified as part of the sexuality bit of that acronym – for asexuality – and as part of the T bit too, for being non-binary. Because asexual and non-binary were never presented as options when I was growing up I went through life not knowing where I fitted in. The sense of liberation and empowerment at finding another 'tribe' in addition to – or more accurately alongside – my autism was amazing. The odd thing about the survey at work was that I felt I didn't belong. I shouldn't answer the questions or tick the boxes. They weren't me, even though I knew they *are* me. There were some complicated emotions and allegiances for this little person and, I imagine, a great many others. Gender identity and sexuality have so much bound up in terms of identity.

I always feel that I need to justify my gender identity – 'I used to have a shaved head and wear flannelette check shirts and Blundstone boots', or, 'People always get my gender mixed up', or, 'I only wear feminine things because I like flower patterns and colourful jewellery. I don't wear heels and I only wear make-up if I'm talking to an audience of over a hundred people!' Gender is something people have an opinion on, and a lot of the time it is an unhelpful opinion. Even now I feel the need to justify my own identity because of those opinions from others, not all of which are intentionally disrespectful, despite how they come across and impact my sense of who I am.

In my understanding, gender is how you feel when you think about yourself. What other people think is irrelevant and nobody should ever have to justify their own identity. For me, my gender is 'me'. I don't feel 'boy' or 'girl'. In fact, I can't really say what those things would feel like. The self-consciousness strikes all the time.

And there is that again, that 'time'. I think a fair number of us are changing all the time in terms of gender identity and sexuality. We are coming out of a historical period where sexuality and gender have been quite strictly proscribed through social 'norms' and rules, and, let's face it, through a fair amount or prejudice and violence too. Even now when things seem to be improving, there are those persistent legacy attitudes threatening to deny people the right to be themselves and express themselves in the way they are.

Throughout my life, kids have questioned my gender identity. Often a sort of bullying challenge is 'What are you? Are you a boy or a girl?' This used to really get to me and I felt powerless, but angry. Why did it matter if I was a boy or a girl? I am a person, not a specific gender type. It still happens now and I say 'Neither. I'm "me"' and smile at them. Inwardly, I'm still feeling attacked and scared but I am also representing trans and gender-diverse people in my own little way.

When I was a teenager, gender and sexuality were very strictly enforced, mostly by the 'gender police' of the school bullies and often through unspoken norms and judgements from adults. I never went to a school dance. That's not the worst deprivation of course, but the reasons behind me not even considering going to such an event were around the twin weapons of homophobia and transphobia. I pretended to be heterosexual for years, even to the extent of turning one of my male friends into my ex-partner to fool a housemate who was sexist and homophobic. As an autistic person, I struggled to lie but I feared for my safety if I told the truth. This horrifies me in hindsight and terrifies me that these attitudes of hatred and violence still continue.

A huge number of autistic people also identify as part of the LGBTQIA+ umbrella. There is emerging evidence that strongly suggests that there is a significantly increased percentage of non-heterosexual, non-binary gender identities among autistic people compared with neurotypical people.

I think identity – whatever part of your experience it relates to – is such a strong thing. Autistics and members of other identities can have a very strong self-identity, supported by like-minded people and genuine allies. Or we can have our identity squashed out of us through ignorance and bigotry or just the application of incorrect assumptions which we are too hurt by or frightened of to challenge. For me, the various facets of my identity which I have gathered over many difficult years are a precious thing. I would really like a world where people could express themselves and live openly and proudly in their own identity.

I am neither a boy nor a girl but I am a 'me', and an autistic and non-binary and asexual one at that, and I have a mental illness and I identify with women as I have been on the receiving end of misogyny and abuse and I have seen others be attacked by this as well. My identity changes and grows as I travel through life. I am so glad after many years of keeping things secret – even from myself at times – that I get to be my own unique me. That is my wish for everyone else too. 🙶

Positive self-identity is hugely important for trans and gender-diverse autistic people. Pride enables us to navigate the world with confidence and a sense that we actually do matter.

However, there are lots of risk factors which can strip away our sense of pride. These include:

∞ Transphobia

∞ Ableism

∞ Discrimination in the workplace

∞ Negative responses from family and friends

∞ Negative response from partner

∞ Negative representation of trans and autistic people in the media and popular culture

∞ Discrimination in educational settings

∞ Bigotry in politics and from elected officials.

Some of these risk factors do not have an easy solution and are beyond our power to 'fix'. However, there are some protective factors that we can engage with and put in place which will help address the risk factors and enable us to build our sense of pride. These include:

∞ Positive affirmation from family, friends, family of choice

∞ Advocacy and activism

∞ Positive representation in the media/popular culture

∞ Supportive partner

∞ An existing sense of self-confidence

∞ Role models and mentors

∞ Positive legislation and support from elected officials

∞ Supportive workplace

∞ Supportive educational settings

∞ Connections with autistic and trans peer group

∞ Involvement with organizations that support autistic people and trans people (e.g. QLife or A Gender Agenda)

∞ Involvement with events that promote pride (Sydney Gay and Lesbian Mardi Gras, Autscape, etc.).

If your life is filled with protective factors for pride then that will go a huge way to developing your positive self-identity and sense of autistic and trans pride. Pride is a big protective factor in and of itself. Pride can be a counter to a number of challenges, including low self-esteem, self-hatred, suicidal ideation and internalized ableism and transphobia.

Living with your transgender self

Once you have made the decision to transition from your assigned gender at birth and become the individual you always were but had not previously realized or 'set free', you will be open to a number of experiences not previously encountered.

❝ {WENN} Church life was very important to me and was a huge part of my everyday life. However, as my self-knowledge and identity changed, from not knowing I was autistic to knowing, then to believing I was a butch lesbian and eventually to that lightbulb moment of recognition that I was trans, my church life also changed radically. First I came to the reality of being autistic as an adult of 42 years, having gone through life knowing I was different, but not knowing why, then to having both family and friends question my autism, and this changed many of the relational dynamics at that time; to working so hard to build a successful marriage as a 'heterosexual' person and feeling like such a failure as the reality dawned I just was not able to; to coming to terms with my sexual attraction to women and being totally freaked out, but then moving towards an acceptance of this (so I must be a butch lesbian) but still not finding a community where I felt at home; to that day in late 2012 when I began to build the understanding that I might not be a person more at home with the idea of 'middlesex' but I might be a guy! Although I didn't begin my travels, actively, towards my gender transition until 2013, the journey itself began way before this. I just didn't have clear signposts for it, nor the language and knowledge to understand it, or where it was leading me.

You might identify with my story or you might not, but coming into that place of feeling proud of who you are is a journey for us all, even if it takes different paths to reach our destination. Church and my faith are still very important to me, I just haven't had the courage yet to face these head on. Faith is fine, it can hold a place in your life that is private and you might not want or need to share it. But church, well, I'd like to check out some places of worship locally to me, but I don't want to risk opening myself and all I have become to have others trample what is so precious to me. I'll probably get there, eventually, but I'm not ready yet. Being proud is our right, yes, but choosing when to be proud and out there can take time and needs careful negotiation. Don't be in a hurry, check things out first. Share with trusted others and build the right community around yourself, one you feel connected to and at home with. 〞

Change of hair salon? If you are non-binary and believe you can get your hair cut anywhere, you are probably happier to go to a 'unisex' hairdresser. If you are a trans woman you probably prefer a ladies' hairdresser. If it's your first time having a hair cut in a different hair salon to those in your past, it might be very uncomfortable the first few times you need to do this, but it gets better.

Strengths

Feeling good about yourself is one of your strengths, even though you might not have thought about it in this way. When we feel good we are more likely to be confident and, therefore, more capable. Autism is often thought about in terms of negative impact on our lives but the reality is we are very focused people and can 'hone in' on an interest and make it a passion. We can then use our passion wisely and well. We can enjoy sharing our learning with others and this in turn can help us to feel useful. Unlocking your own strengths and passions could be an asset in finding your place in the world, if you haven't already. It also means we heal better if we feel good about who we are.

Seeing ourselves in the light of all we are does not have to set us up to fail, when we view ourselves in light of our strengths. Traditionally, autism has only been seen in the light of our deficits, but this isn't the whole picture and it leaves all the colour off the canvas. We are so good at so many things.

66 {WENN} I have a very spiky profile with my executive functioning ability being at the lower end of the spectrum of ability and my love and knowledge for birds being at the higher end. I know I need support with any executive functioning priorities, such as knowing what comes first, then next, then after! I also find it hard to read faces, as well as the intentions of others, and these areas of difficulty can impact negatively on my own expectations and the expectations of others. But owning our difficulties and accepting support when and where we can is part of life for all of us and, as a community, only serves to build us all up. 99

So, once we have the support we need, we can navigate our day in ways that work best for us. Sometimes we can use technology to help us.

66 {WENN} I have a smart watch that lets me know programmed appointments. It also helps with medication times,

my heart rate and how much exercise I'm getting! I also utilize the support of friends, family and work colleagues. 99

Understanding our needs is crucial to enabling us to make the most of the support on offer, then navigate towards the future we hope for. In our current Western climate and culture, this future is in reach for us. We are aware that it isn't the case for everyone, but we hope that this chapter helps to explain some of our 'autism' stuff and at least can give each of us a hope that we are not on our own!

CHAPTER 8

Mental Health

Reasons why mental health issues among the LGBTQIA+ population are so high is often more to do with societal acceptance, support and the real accommodations that we need not being forthcoming.

Autism and mental health

While autism is not itself a mental illness, it is very common for autistic people to have a mental illness. Autistic people are particularly prone to depression and anxiety but can also have any of the other mental illness diagnoses. Autism can make a mental illness appear different and a mental illness can conversely make autism present atypically. Autistic people often struggle accessing support, including accurate diagnoses of both their mental illness condition and their autism. Mental health clinicians often lack training in autism which can compound these issues. Autism spectrum conditions are neurological conditions and are classified under the area of neurodevelopment. Evidence suggests that there is a genetic loading to autism, meaning that autistic people are born with their autism but can acquire a mental health condition.

Autistic people are also often targeted by bullies and may have post-traumatic stress disorder.

Some interesting points

∞ 'Gender identity disorder' was changed in the updated *Diagnostic and Statistical Manual of Mental Disorders, fifth edition* (American Psychiatric Association, 2013) to 'gender dysphoria' in 2013.[1]

∞ In the *International Classification of Diseases, 11th revision*, 'gender identity disorder' was changed to the term 'gender in-congruence'.[2]

∞ It's unfortunate that these terms are in manuals for 'diseases', but we look at it as 'dis-ease' or lack of body and/or mind ease.

∞ Suicide rates are completely different for pre- and post-support, especially for medical transition.[3]

Trans and gender-diverse mental health

Trans and gender-diverse people experience mental health conditions at a high rate, including depression, anxiety and suicidal ideation. This often relates to trauma experienced

---

1 https://www.theravive.com/therapedia/gender-dysphoria-dsm--5-302.85-(f64.9)
2 www.tandfonline.com/doi/full/10.1080/09688080.2018.1544770
3 www.nytimes.com/2018/04/09/opinion/pentagon-transgender.html

through transphobic bullying and violence. Many trans and gender-diverse people have been on the receiving end of transphobic abuse since childhood. Coupled with being autistic, this can lead to post-traumatic stress.

What is post-traumatic stress disorder?

Post-traumatic stress disorder (PTSD) is a particular set of reactions that can develop in people who have been through a traumatic event which threatened their life or safety, or that of others around them. This could be a car or other serious accident, physical or sexual assault, hate crime, war or torture, or disasters such as bushfires or floods. As a result, the person experiences feelings of intense fear, helplessness or horror.

People with PTSD often experience feelings of panic or extreme fear, similar to the fear they felt during the traumatic event. A person with PTSD experiences four main types of difficulties:

∞ When an individual re-experiences a traumatic event, they 'actually' relive the events again, as if they were happening to them now. This may be triggered by a memory, which is reoccurring, often vividly visual. Sometimes it's via dreams (nightmares). They will feel the event both physically and emotionally. At times a person will show the signs associated with extreme anxiety, such as sweating, heart palpitations, and panic.

∞ The above may cause an individual to feel like they can't 'switch off' and sleep may not be available to them. They may be irritable, irrational, find it difficult to focus and be constantly on the alert. Individuals experiencing this will be easily startled and vigilant because they are in fight or flight mode.

∞ Individuals will be avoidant, not wanting to be reminded of the trauma. They may purposely avoid any event, person, place, thoughts and/or feelings associated with that trauma or event. They do so to try to ward off unwanted pain!

∞ Some individuals build up an armour around themselves (emotional armour) by distancing themselves. This causes feelings of numbness and disconnection so an individual acts as if they are not interested in a topic or they may quickly lose interest and change the topic. Daily activities and self-care may take a back seat. Individuals may isolate themselves and avoid friends and family. They may feel emotionally flat and numb.

Trauma and autism go hand in hand. Autism predisposes us to trauma simply because the world we all live in often doesn't accommodate autistic thinking and behaviour. When a baby is born a mother/caregiver usually bonds to the child through mutual connection. Connection is formed via touch, eye contact, recognition of emotive states, smiles and responses to perceived need. If a caregiver can't initiate connection to the child via traditional means (reaching out and feedback from child) they may feel inadequate, perceive the child doesn't like them, withdraw from the child and so on. Autistic individuals develop the entire range of attachment (including disorganized attachment).[4]

> Clinicians suspect that the condition [autism] increases the risk for certain kinds of trauma, such as bullying and other forms of abuse. Yet few studies have investigated that possibility or the psychological aftermath of such trauma, including PTSD. (Gravitz, 2018, p.2)

In autism, there is significantly weaker connectivity between the amygdala and numerous brain regions that are implicated in social communication and language deficits, as well as repetitive behaviours. More specifically, autistic individuals have weaker connectivity between the amygdala and the medial prefrontal cortex, bilateral temporal lobe, striatum, thalamus, cingulate cortex and cerebellum. This is important because understanding and accommodating social communication requires many brain regions to work together. When a caregiver attempts to hug the child or talk gently, this is usually welcomed in a non-autistic child. But in autism, the hug maybe experienced as suffocating and the calm voice as thunder. Although the reasons for attachment in autism are as usual as for any other child, the way this is appropriated will be different. Recognizing autism early and helping caregivers establish the type of attachment that is secure, consistent and autism friendly will go a long way to preventing trauma. Building an understanding of interoception and object permanence is needed for maintenance, resilience and emotional regulation.

---

4   https://journals.sagepub.com/doi/full/10.1177/2516103218816707

Strategies to promote good mental health

There are a number of strategies to promote good mental health and to address issues. Some of these work well for trans and gender-diverse autistic people. These are detailed below.

Social support

Being able to talk to trusted friends and family (either biological or family of choice) is a key element of maintaining good mental health. It is a good thing and a sign of strength to ask for help.

Accessing support services

There are a range of services which can support you and your mental health. These include QLife (based in Australia and LGBTQIA+ specific), Lifeline (based in Australia), the National Suicide Hotline (based in the USA) and the Samaritans (based in the UK). All these offer confidential telephone counselling services and some also offer online (typed) support. You can talk to a counsellor or psychologist to work through traumatic events or to manage anxiety and learn some strategies. You can ask for recommendations of mental health workers in your area who friends or family members have used and find helpful. It can be good to ask other trans autistic people for recommendations. Some clinicians are fantastic but some are not, so it's good to get a heads up about who will most likely be helpful if possible.

Be aware that you are not alone and that many others are experiencing similar things to you. Feeling connected to others in the trans and gender-diverse and autistic communities can really help. There are groups online, blogs and books by and for trans and gender-diverse autistic people. We are a vibrant and strong community and most members of this community are focused on positives and support for others.

Mindfulness

Mindfulness practice can be very positive in terms of maintaining mental health and well-being. Mindfulness is based in meditation and helps enable people to be in the present moment, tackling only the issues at hand and not dwelling on the past or fixating on worries about the future. There are a number of mindfulness apps including Smiling Mind. Autistic author Dr Emma Goodall has a website focusing on mindfulness.[5]

Suicidal ideation

LGBTQIA+ people and autistic people are at significant risk of suicidal ideation and suicide. There are a range of reasons for this, including bullying and abuse, ableism and transphobia. Autistic people have a significantly lower life expectancy to the general population, and a strong contributor to this is suicide (Autism Cooperative Research Centre[6]). Belonging to both the autism and transgender communities can be seen to compound the risk of suicidal ideation and suicide. It is important to be aware of the increased risks and seek assistance where necessary.

---

5   https://mindfulbodyawareness.com/interoception
6   www.autismcrc.com.au

Protective factors in relation to suicidal ideation for autistic and trans and gender-diverse people include:

∞ Supportive and strong relationships with family and friends

∞ Completed medical transition (if transition is desired)

∞ Effective mental health care and health care

∞ Connection to trans and autistic communities

∞ Pride in one's own gender identity

∞ Autistic pride.

Self-awareness and acceptance

We hope you have found this book helpful. Trans and gender-diverse autistic people have the right to live their lives as they choose and to be themselves. We inhabit a world where trans and gender-diverse and autistic experience is devalued and invalidated and people face discrimination, ableism and transphobia. This is not okay. We want a better world where our experience is valued and we can be open and free about who we really are.

So, rather than hide who you are and battle on alone, please reach out to a trusted friend, your general practitioner, online community or counsellor. You do not need to struggle on your own. There is a place for acceptance and embracing those rights, which are yours, that lead to a path for transitioning/

embracing your gender identity. So many mental and physical health benefits come from feeling good and connected to who you are. These also enable you to access a sense of high personal autonomy and lower your likelihood of poor mental health outcomes. Learning difficulties and some of those associated issues that can make it harder to reach out (the perceived need that you have to be able to read and write well to access support) are also more common for us and can compound and delay social connections, but don't let these fears get in your way.

If you don't feel confident to chat about the things that are happening to you, again, take your time to find a way that supports you in communicating what you need to – this is really important. We have autistic friends who type, others who draw and paint, some who perform in song or dance or drama and express their voice; it's about what works for you. Each of us has a different story and each of us is unique, but together we are stronger and can weave a cloak that covers and protects us from those harsh elements that come with the differing seasons of our lives. The good news? Winter is only a time for the preparation before Spring. We cannot see this work, often going on underground. But once Spring is allowed to do her work, then Summer can take over and they can join together to enable the colourful awakening of fragrant blooms that breathe further life into all. Autism and gender diversity are so beautiful!

References

Chapter 1

American Psychiatric Association (2013) *Diagnostic and Statistical Manual of Mental Disorders, fifth edition* (DSM-5). Washington, DC: APA.

Craig, L., Trundle, G. & Stringer, I. (2017) 'Differentiating between pathological demand avoidance and antisocial personality disorder: A case study.' *Journal of Intellectual Disabilities and Offending Behaviour*, 8, 13–27. doi: 10.1108/JIDOB-07-2016-0013.

Furfaro, H. (2019) *Study Strengthens Autism's Curious Link to Gender Variance*. Spectrum Research News. www.spectrumnews.org/news/study-strengthens-autisms-curious-link-gender-variance.

Ghosh, A., Ray, A. & Basu, A. (2017) 'Oppositional defiant disorder: Current insight.' *Psychology Research and Behavior Management*, 10, 353–367. doi:10.2147/PRBM.S120582.

Gillberg, C., Gillberg, I.C., Thompson, L., Biskupsto, R. & Billstedt, E. (2015) 'Extreme ("pathological") demand avoidance in autism: A general population study in the Faroe Islands.' *European Child & Adolescent Psychiatry*, 24(8) 979–984.

Gravitz, L. (2018) *At the Intersection of Autism and Trauma*. Spectrum Research News. www.spectrumnews.org/features/deep-dive/intersection-autism-trauma.

Lai, M-C., Lombardo, M.V. & Baron-Cohen, S. (2013) 'Autism.' *The Lancet*, 383(9920) 896–910. https://doi.org/10.1016/S0140-6736(13)61539-1.

Lawson, W. (2000) *Understanding and Working with the Spectrum of Autism*. London: Jessica Kingsley Publishers.

Lawson, W. (2011) *The Passionate Mind: How Individuals with Autism Learn*. London: Jessica Kingsley Publishers.

Loomes, R., Hull, L. & Mandy, W.P.L. (2017) 'What is the male ratio in autism spectrum disorder? A systematic review and meta-analysis.' *Journal of the American Academy of Child and Adolescent Psychiatry*, 56(6) 466–474.

Murray, D.M., Lesser, M. & Lawson, W. (2005) 'Attention, monotropism and the diagnostic criteria for autism.' *Autism*, 9(2) 139–152.

Newson, E., Le Marechal, K. & David, C. (2003) 'Pathological demand avoidance syndrome: A necessary distinction within the pervasive developmental disorders.' *Archive of Disease in Childhood*, 88, 595–600.

O'Nions, E., Christie, P., Gould, J., Viding, E. & Happé, F. (2014a) 'Development of the "Extreme Demand Avoidance Questionnaire" (EDA-Q): Preliminary observations on a trait measure for pathological demand avoidance.' *Journal of Child Psychology and Psychiatry*, 55(7) 758–768.

O'Nions, E., Viding, E., Greven, C.U., Ronald, A. & Happé, F. (2014b) 'Pathological demand avoidance: Exploring the behavioural profile.' *Autism*, 18, 538–544.

O'Nions, E., Gould, J., Christie, P., Gillberg, C., Viding, E. & Happé, F. (2016) 'Identifying features of "pathological demand avoidance" using the Diagnostic Interview for Social and Communication Disorders.' *European Child & Adolescent Psychiatry*, 25(4) 407–419.

Chapter 2

Adams, N., Hitomi, M. & Moody, C. (2017) 'Varied reports of adult transgender suicidality: Synthesizing and describing the peer-reviewed and gray literature.' *Transgender Health*, 2, 60–75.

American Psychiatric Association (2013) *Diagnostic and Statistical Manual of Mental Disorders, fifth edition* (DSM-5). Washington, DC: APA.

Bailey, L., Ellis, S. & McNeil, J. (2014) 'Suicide risk in the UK trans population and the role of gender transition in decreasing suicidal ideation and suicide attempt.' *Mental Health Review Journal*, 19(4) 209–220.

Cassidy, S. (2015) *Suicidality in Autism: Risk and Prevention*. Centre for Research in Psychology Behaviour and Achievement, Coventry University.

Gravitz, L. (2018) *At the Intersection of Autism and Trauma*. Spectrum News. www.spectrumnews.org/features/deep-dive/intersection-autism-trauma.

Heylens, G., Aspeslagh, L., Dierickx, J., Baetens, K. *et al.* (2018) 'The co-occurrence of gender dysphoria and autism spectrum disorder in adults: An analysis of cross-sectional and clinical chart data.' *Journal of Autism and Developmental Disorders*, 48(6) 2217–2223. doi:10.1007/s10803-018-3480-6.

Lai, M-C., Lombardo, M.V. & Baron-Cohen, S. (2013) 'Autism.' *The Lancet*, 383(9920) 896–910. https://doi.org/10.1016/S0140-6736(13)61539-1.

Lever, A.G. & Geurts, H.M. (2016) 'Psychiatric co-occurring symptoms and disorders in young, middle-aged, and older adults with autism spectrum disorder.' *Journal of Autism and Developmental Disorders*, 46(6) 1916–1930. https://doi.org/10.1007/s10803-016-2722-8.

Nobili, A., Glazebrook, C., Bouman, W.P., Glidden, D. *et al.* (2018) 'Autistic traits in treatment-seeking transgender adults.' *Journal of Autism and Developmental Disorders*, 48(12) 3984–3994. https://doi.org/10.1007/s10803-018-3557-2.

Stagg, S.D. & Vincent, J. (2019) 'Autistic traits in individuals self-defining as transgender or nonbinary.' *European Psychiatry*, 61, 17–22. doi:10.1016/j.eurpsy.2019.06.003.

Strang, J.F. (2018) *Why We Need to Respect Sexual Orientation, Gender Diversity in Autism*. Spectrum News. www.spectrumnews.org/opinion/viewpoint/need-respect-sexual-orientation-gender-diversity-autism.

Strang, J.F., Janssen, A., Tishelman, A. & Leibowitz, S.F. (2018) 'Revisiting the link: Evidence of the rates of autism in studies of gender diverse individuals.' *Journal of the American Academy of Child and Adolescent Psychiatry*, 57(11) 885–887. doi:10.1016/j.jaac.2018.04.023.

Strang, J.F., Kenworthy, L., Dominska, A., Sokoloff, J. (2014) 'Increased gender variance in autism spectrum disorders and attention deficit hyperactivity disorder.' *Archives of Sexual Behavior*, 43(8) 1525–1533. https://doi.org/10.1007/s10508-014-0285-3.

Tourjeé, D. (2017) *The Girl's Guide to Changing your Gender*. Available at www. vice.com/en_us/article/43e899/male-to-female-transition-guide.

Van Der Miesen, A.I.R., Hurley, H. & De Vries, A.C.L. (2016) 'Gender dysphoria and autism spectrum disorder: A narrative review.' *International Review of Psychiatry*, 28(1) 70–80. doi:10.3109/09540261.2015.1111199.

Chapter 3

Lawson, W. & Lawson, B. (2017) *Transitioning Together: One Couple's Journey of Gender and Identity Discovery*. London: Jessica Kingsley Publishers.

Chapter 5

American Psychiatric Association (2013) *Diagnostic and Statistical Manual of Mental Disorders, fifth edition* (DSM-5). Washington, DC: APA.

Asperger, H. (1992) 'Autistic Psychopathy in Childhood.' In U. Frith (ed.), *Autism and Asperger Syndrome*, pp.37–92. Cambridge: Cambridge University Press.

Attwood, T. (2007) *The Complete Guide to Asperger's Syndrome*. London: Jessica Kingsley Publishers.

Baldwin, S., Costley, D. & Warren, A. (2013) *We Belong: The Experiences, Aspirations and Needs of Adults with Asperger's Disorder and High Functioning Autism*. Australia: Autism Spectrum Australia (Aspect).

Cage, E., Di Monaco, J. & Newell, V. (2018) 'Experiences of autism acceptance and mental health in autistic adults.' *Journal of Autism and Developmental Disorders*, 48, 473–484.

Carpenter, B., Happé, F. & Egerton, J. (2019) *Girls and Autism: Educational, Family and Personal Perspectives*. Abingdon, Oxfordshire: Taylor & Francis.

Cassidy, S., Bradley, L., Shaw, R. & Baron-Cohen, S. (2018) 'Risk markers for suicidality in autistic adults.' *Molecular Autism*, 9(1) 42.

Constantino, J.N. & Charman, T. (2012) 'Gender bias, female resilience, and the sex ratio in autism.' *Journal of the American Academy of Child and Adolescent Psychiatry*, 51(8) 756–758. https://doi.org/10.1016/j.jaac.2012.05.017.

Cox, K.H., Quinnies, K.M., Eschendroeder, A., Didrick, P.M., Eugster, E.A. & Rissman, E.F. (2015) 'Number of X-chromosome genes influences social behavior and vasopressin gene expression in mice.' *Psychoneuroendocrinology*, 51, 271–281. doi:10.1016/j.psyneuen.2014.10.010.

Eaton, J. (2017) *A Guide to Mental Health Issues in Girls and Young Women on the Autism Spectrum: Diagnosis, Intervention and Family Support*. London: Jessica Kingsley Publishers.

Edmonds, P. (2015) *The Colorful Language of Chameleons*. National Geographic. www.nationalgeographic.com/magazine/2015/09/chameleons-color-change-mimicry-science.

European Society of Endocrinology (2018) 'Transgender brains are more like their desired gender from an early age.' ScienceDaily. www.sciencedaily.com/releases/2018/05/180524112351.htm.

Feinstein, A. (2010) *A History of Autism: Conversations with the Pioneers*. London: Wiley.

Gerland, G. (1997) *A Real Person: Life on the Outside*. London: Souvenir Press.

Goodall, E. (2019) *Understanding the Autism Spectrum*. South Australian Government Department for Education Disability, Policy & Programs. www.education.sa.gov.au/sites/default/files/understanding-the-autism-spectrum.pdf?acsf_files_redirect.

Gopher, D., Armony, L. & Greenspan, Y. (2000) 'Switching tasks and attention policies.' *Journal of Experimental Psychology: General*, 129, 308–339.

Head, A.M., McGillivray, J.A. & Stokes, M.A. (2014) 'Gender differences in emotionality and sociability in children with autism spectrum disorders.' *Molecular Autism*, 5, 19. doi:10.1186/2040-2392-5-19.

Heyworth, M. (2018) #Take the Mask Off (but what if I don't know how?) – Reframing Autism Blog, 26 August, www.reframingautism.com.au/takethemaskoff.

Holliday-Willey, L. (1999) *Pretending to be Normal*. London: Jessica Kingsley Publishers.

Howlin, P. & Moss, P. (2012) 'Adults with autism spectrum disorders.' *Canadian Journal of Psychiatry*, 57(5) 275–283.

Hull, L., Petrides, K.V., Allison, C., Smith, P. *et al.* (2017) '"Putting on my best normal": Social camouflaging in adults with autism spectrum conditions.' *Journal of Autism and Developmental Disorders*, 47(8) 2519–2534. https://doi.org/10.1007/s10803-017-3166-5.

Lai, M.C., Lombardo, M.V., Ruigrok, A.N., Chakrabarti, B. *et al.* (2017) 'Quantifying and exploring camouflaging in men and women with autism.' *Autism*, 21, 690–702.

Lawson, W. (1998) *Life Behind Glass.* Lismore, NSW: Southern Cross University Press.

Lawson, W. (2011) *The Passionate Mind.* London: Jessica Kingsley Publishers.

Lawson, W. (2017) 'Women and girls with autism: A profile.' *Journal of Intellectual Disability – Diagnosis and Treatment*, 5, 90–95.

Lawson, W. & Dombroski, B. (2017) 'Problems with object permanence: Rethinking traditional beliefs associated with poor theory of mind in autism.' *Journal of Intellectual Disability – Diagnosis and Treatment*, 5, 1–6.

Lawson, W. & Lawson, B. (2017) *Transitioning Together: One Couple's Journey of Gender and Identity Discovery.* London: Jessica Kingsley Publishers.

Livingston, L.A., Shah, P. & Happé, F. (2019) 'Compensatory strategies below the behavioural surface in autism: A qualitative study.' *The Lancet, Psychiatry*, 6(9) 766–777.

Murray, D.K., Lesser, M. & Lawson, W. (2005) 'Attention, monotropism & the diagnostic criteria for autism.' *Autism*, 9(2) 139–156.

National Autistic Society (2019) www.autism.org.uk/about.aspx.

Nirode, V. (2018) 'Why I Fake Being "Normal" – and Other Women with Autism Do, Too.' www.healthline.com/health/autism/how-women-camouflage-autism#1.

Parker, R. & Aggleton, P. (2003) 'HIV and AIDS-related stigma and discrimination: A conceptual framework and implications for action.' *Social Science and Medicine*, 57(1) 13–24.

Platzman Weinstock, C. (2018) *The Hidden Danger of Suicide in Autism.* Spectrum Research News. www.spectrumnews.org.

Porges, S.W. (2004) 'Neuroception: A subconscious system for detecting threats and safety.' *Zero to Three*, 24(5) 19–24.

Preston, D. (2011) 'The power of language regard: Discrimination, classification, comprehension and production.' *Dialectologia* (Special issue), 2, 9–33.

Ronch, J. & Thomas, W. (2009) 'Words matter.' *Journal on Jewish Aging*, 3(1) 1–4.

Troxell-Whitman, Z. & Cage, E. (2019) 'Understanding the reasons, contexts and costs of camouflaging for autistic adults.' *Journal of Autism and Developmental Disorders*, 49(10) 1899–1911.

Turk, D.S. cited in Sparrow, M. (2020) *Spectrums: Autistic Transgender People in their Own Words*. London: Jessica Kingsley Publishers.

Wood, R. (2019) 'Autism, intense interests and support in school: From wasted efforts to shared understandings.' *Educational Review*. doi:10.1080/00131911.2019.1566213.

Chapter 6

Fletcher-Watson, S. & Happé, F. (2019) *A New Introduction to Psychological Theory and Current Debate*. London: Routledge.

Gerland, G. (2003) *A Real Person: Living Life on the Outside*. London: Souvenir Press.

Lawson, W. (2000) *Life behind Glass*. London: Jessica Kingsley Publishers.

Lawson, W. (2011) *The Passionate Mind*. London: Jessica Kingsley Publishers.

Lawson, W. & Lawson, B. (2017) *Transitioning Together: One Couple's Journey of Gender and Identity Discovery*. London: Jessica Kingsley Publishers.

Purkis, J. (2006) *Finding a Different Kind of Normal*. London: Jessica Kingsley Publishers.

Veldorale-Griffin, A. (2014) 'Transgender parents and their adult children's experiences of disclosure and transition.' *Journal of GLBT Family Studies*, 10, 475–501. https://doi.org/10.1080/1550428X.2013.866063.

Chapter 7

Blair, C. (2006) 'How similar are fluid cognition and general intelligence? A developmental neuroscience perspective on fluid cognition as an aspect of human cognitive ability.' *Behavioral and Brain Sciences*, 29, 109–125.

Dawson, M., Soulières, I., Morton, A.G. & Mottron, L. (2007) 'The level and nature of autistic intelligence.' *Psychological Science*, 18(8) 657–662.

Chapter 8

American Psychiatric Association (2013) *Diagnostic and Statistical Manual of Mental Disorders, fifth edition* (DSM-5). Washington, DC: APA.

Gravitz, L. (2018) *At the Intersection of Autism and Trauma*. Spectrum Research News. www.spectrumnews.org/features/deep-dive/inter-section-autism-trauma.

Index

Index